Lost in Translation

Common Errors in
Chinese-English Translation

YANG WEN

LifeRich Publishing is a registered trademark of
The Reader's Digest Association, Inc.

LifeRich Publishing books may be ordered through booksellers or by contacting:

LifeRich Publishing
1663 Liberty Drive
Bloomington, IN 47403
www.liferichpublishing.com
1 (888) 238-8637

ISBN: 978-1-4897-0899-1 (sc)
ISBN: 978-1-4897-0900-4 (hc)
ISBN: 978-1-4897-0898-4 (e)

Library of Congress Control Number: 2016912684

Print information available on the last page.

LifeRich Publishing rev. date: 10/18/2016

To you who find fun in translation

Contents

Acknowledgments

It all started with a gentle tap on my shoulder one afternoon in the spring of 1970, my first year at Tianjin Xinkai High. Mrs. Qu motioned me to follow her.

Two minutes later, I found myself in the Dean's Office. Two city officials were behind a large desk. They studied me for a while before announcing that they were sending me to a boarding school, Tianjin Foreign Languages School, a prestigious school, which was the envy of many kids, as well as their parents.

Thus, I took my first step on the long and rewarding journey to be a linguist.

I owe who I am today to my teachers at Tianjin Foreign Languages School in China: Dai laoshi, Yang laoshi, Qi laoshi, Tu laoshi, Wang laoshi, and the entire Class 70-2. Together, we laughed, misbehaved, and, of course, learned English—a lot of it.

Special thanks must go to my professors and dear friends at Georgetown University (USA): Dean Cloke, Father Curren, Dr. John Hirsh, Dr. Brown, Dr. McKewn, Dr. Spendelow, and Dora Richardson. They helped me in so many ways. They instilled in me a profound understanding of American culture, a valuable background for a better understanding of the English language.

I want to thank Chris Crocoll, supervisor of the Chinese section at the Foreign Service Institute (FSI) of US Department of State. On a rainy afternoon in the fall of 1995, I made a self-invited visit to his office. What was originally meant to be a here-is-my-résumé visit became a two-hour conversation on language, language teaching, and much more.

Two weeks later, I was a language and culture instructor at FSI, my first step to a long, rewarding translation career.

I also owe my debt to my colleagues at FSI, who generously shared their insights on language, culture, and translation. To Xu Huijuan and Wedan Swanson, with whom I shared an office for nearly a decade, where brilliant ideas on the nuance of Chinese and English languages were discussed; to Chen Ji, whose profound understanding of language issues inspired me and whose unassuming attitude served (and still does) as the role model for me in ways far beyond language teaching.

Tons of thanks go to my colleagues at Science Applications International Corporation (SAIC): James, Frank, Jane, Sandy, Tom, and little Yang. I learned a lot from their insight, style, and often beautiful translations.

Many thanks go to Caleb, Patrick, Ann, Dieu, and Kerri, members of my other team at LEIDOS. I took mental notes of language nuances during our conversations, some of which became part of this book.

I must thank Heidi in particular for giving me the challenging and rewarding opportunity to be a quality control (QC) linguist, a position that allowed me to look at translation through a different lens.

My heartfelt thanks go to Wendy Abraham, author of *Chinese for Dummies* and a good friend of mine. My idea of writing this book started after receiving an e-mail from her, asking me to be the technical editor for her *Dummies* book. In a unique way, she inspired me. And with her brilliant suggestions for this book's title, her inspiration comes full circle.

I must also thank River, my dog. Many of the *aha* moments came to me during our walks around the neighborhood.

Of course, the book would not have been possible without the remarkable editorial staff at LifeRich Publishing. They caught errors, smoothed edges, and asked tough questions.

Finally, I am thankful for my wife, who has supported me in more ways than a husband could ask for; and for my daughter, Laura, whose challenging questions often make me think twice.

One day, on our drive home, I commented that after checking an ID, a guard would say, "Have a good day!" There were no better ways of translating it, I insisted, than a simple 谢谢, which is what a Chinese would say in a similar circumstance. "Not really," my daughter replied. "You have to find a way to reflect its unique flavor as well as meaning. 谢谢 isn't enough."

Flavor and meaning!

Isn't it the translation Mount Everest that every linguist aspires to reach?

Introduction

When two languages meet, translation happens.

Years ago, a visiting Chinese scholar asked me to help him out during one of his doctor visits. He didn't speak much English.

"My waist … pain … many days." The Chinese scholar was apparently trying to come up with all the English words he knew.

The doctor looked up from his notepad, trying to make sense of what he heard. I quickly jumped in. "Oh, he meant *lower back*."

The doctor nodded and moved on with his note taking.

One winter evening, Tom, my roommate during my college days at Georgetown University, was waiting for me in front of an ice rink in Washington, DC. As I was crossing the street to join him, I noticed his surprised look.

"我不知道你穿眼镜!" He was looking at my new glasses. "你是说 '戴' 眼镜吧!" I quickly corrected him. But he didn't seem to realize the correction. *Wear* can be rendered both 穿 and 戴 and many more, depending on what you are wearing.

It was not a time for a Chinese lesson anyway. We quickly put on our skates and joined the crowd on the ice rink.

The Chinese scholar obviously was trying to say 腰疼 in English; Tom was trying to say *wear* in Chinese, a translation mode that millions of native Chinese (who are trying to communicate in English) and native English speakers (who are trying to do the same in Chinese) are going through all day, every day, all across the Chinese- and English-speaking worlds.

The *waist pain* and 穿眼镜 episodes are just the tip of the linguistic iceberg of awkward translation.

Does 属于 always translate as *belong to*?

Does 文化 always translate as *culture*?

Does 经济 always translate as *economy*?

And does 矛盾 always translate as *contradiction*?

What if you are presenting your research findings and conclude with the profound observation, *"We should be aware that the contradictions in the IT market are becoming serious!"*

In your mind, you mean, 我们应该注意到IT 市场的矛盾日趋严重!

Do you believe you have made yourself understood, not to mention that you have impressed your boss and coworkers?

One thing is sure, you have successfully confused everybody. The reason: poor choice of the word *contradiction* for 矛盾.

But, you may protest, this is what the dictionaries have for 矛盾!

You are right. But dictionaries can only go so far.

This book is here to pick up where dictionaries left off, by showing you the right word for the right context. *Contradiction,* in many cases, is not 矛盾.

Improper choice of words can cause many golden opportunities to slip away, many opportunities for promotion to be put on hold, and many otherwise excellent papers to be denied, all because of not knowing how to put that critical Chinese expression into English properly.

Once again, to drive home the importance of proper word choice, let's take 文化 as an example. Dictionaries would give you *culture*. But how do you render 他没有文化; 他的文化水平很高; 他的文化背景如何? The word *culture* won't work in these cases.

Better yet, take 经济 (as a noun), for example. Dictionaries would give you *economy*. But how do you translate 他家经济条件很差; 这个厂的经济状况很好; 我家经济收入不多? The word *economy* does not work either.

Let's come back to 矛盾 again. Dictionaries give you *contradiction*. But how do you translate 他们的矛盾很深; 我们之间没有矛盾; 他们常闹矛盾; 不应该把矛盾上交? The word *contradiction* won't help.

If you translate any of these Chinese words according to dictionary definitions, your readers will think twice about your abilities. It is like you are trying to sell a fine product, only to write its name incorrectly.

Many Chinese professionals are frustrated by their lack of ability to put into English exactly what they are trying to say. They have a brilliant idea, only to see it come out clumsily.

Likewise, many English speakers often find their translations bemuse Chinese readers, even though every word is accounted for. The reason: not every word needs to be accounted for.

Do you translate 慢慢吃 as *eat slowly* when you hear your Chinese host say it? 慢慢走 as *walk slowly,* or 慢慢开as *drive slowly* when your Chinese friend is waving you good-bye at the door?

This book is here to help you in your translation, be it a profession or a necessity, such as what the Chinese scholar and Tom went through.

夫如是，一书到手，经营反复，确知其意旨所在，而又摹写其精神，仿佛其语气，然后心悟神解，振笔而书。译成之文，适如其所译而止，而曾无毫发出于其间。夫而后能使阅者所得之意，与观原文无异，则为善译也。[1]

—— 清·马建忠 光绪二十年

[1] http://www.lunwendata.com/thesis/2005/9873.html

"So, what's your Feng Shui?"

Chapter 1

Word Choice Matters

> **Good translation is never a word-for-word translation because it misinterprets the original content and spoils the beauty of its form.**
>
> **--*Étienne Dolet* (French scholar and translator, 1509–1546)**

It is a familiar scene: You come across a Chinese term, look it up in a Chinese-English dictionary or Google it, find its English translation, and plug it into the sentence. Bingo!

But wait! Is that the right word?

Often, there are multiple English word choices for one Chinese term. Is it *valid* or *effective* or *efficient* for 有效? Is it *legal* or *lawful* for 合法? Is it *complex* or *complicated* for 复杂? Is it *assessment* or *evaluation* or *appraisal* for 评估? Is it *relation* or *relationship* for 关系? Is it *flexible, agile, nimble,* or *versatile* for 灵活? Is it *country, nation,* or *state* for 国家? Is it *precision* or *accuracy* for 精确? Is it *jamming* or *interference* for 干扰?

The list can go on and on. Do we use the first choice on the list, assuming it must be the one most-often used? One of my former colleagues believed so, as she was learning English at the time.

Below is a list of Chinese terms, just the tip of the iceberg. They are totally problem-free until one tries to find their corresponding English versions. Appropriate word choice is a constant battle.

Dictionaries can help only so much, not because they are incapable but because they don't have enough space to explain, for example, why *legal* not *lawful* should be used for 合法in a particular context.

The list below, alphabetically in pinyin, tells you why.

A

安全 (an quan): *safe or secure*

Dictionaries list both *safe* and *secure* under 安全. In many cases, the words seem to be used interchangeably: home security/home safety; personal safety/personal security; safety devices/security devices.

While they both mean "free from danger" (没有危险), each one expresses a different sense of 安全 and protection against a different kind of danger.

When someone says, "It is safe to say that we have a deal now," he or she is suggesting the conclusion won't cause any trouble, political or legal.

When one says, "The building is secure," the person is saying that no criminals can get into the building and steal classified information.

When people say, "The building is safe," they are saying the building doesn't have any structural problems that can cause physical harm to people.

But not all 安全 are created equal.

Simply put, *safe*, for 安全, is more about something being free from danger or harm to humans, as in an injury to the head, a cut on the arm, or bruises on the face.

Whereas *secure*, for 安全, is more about something that is free from danger or harm to systems or organizations (even countries), as in information theft, identity theft, a violation of rights, or a breach of national security.

Case in point: shortly after a passenger plane takes off, crew members give a *safety* demonstration (安全演示), not a *security* demonstration, because they are telling passengers how to protect themselves from physical harm during an emergency situation, not how to protect the aircraft flight systems from being damaged by terrorists or operation systems from being hacked.

After the safety demonstration, the crew members recommend you read the 安全说明 in front of you. It reads *Safety Instructions*, not *Security Instructions*.

During my recent trip to China, on a baggage scanning machine in a train station I found 行李安全检查 translated as *Safety Check*.

The translation is correct if it means that the machine checks if your baggage is strong enough, packed to the standards, and wrapped tightly or if any contents are falling out. This, obviously, is not what the scanner is looking for.

The translation is wrong if it means the machine checks if any baggage contains firearms or illegal drugs. In this case, 安全 should be *security*.

Examples:

➢ 人身安全
Personal safety is often about protection against physical harm. Personal safety devices often (not always) include pepper spray, a helmet, safety glasses, and the like.

Personal security is about protection of one's rights. As the Universal Declaration of Human Rights states: "Everyone has the right to life, liberty, and security of person."

➤ 国家安全
National security is preferred, never *national safety*, because this term is about reducing the country's risk of being attacked, militarily or nonmilitarily.

➤ 交通安全
Road traffic safety is the accurate term, not *road traffic security*, because it refers to reducing people's risk of being killed or injured.

➤ 办公室安全
Office safety is more about reducing workplace accidents, such as falling on a slippery floor or a piece of ceiling falling on one's head.

Office security is more about safeguarding office information and allowing no unauthorized persons into the office.

➤ 安全问题
Safety issues refers to injury and death.
Security issues is about information, national interests, and commercial secrets.

➤ 系统安全
System security refers to protecting the system from being hacked. Physical harm to personnel by the system is not the issue.

➤ 施工安全
Construction safety relates to protecting workers from injuries. Theft of construction secrets is not the issue.

B

保证 (bao zheng): *ensure, assure, guarantee*

These terms mean roughly the same thing. Dictionaries use one to explain the other, but they are not 100 percent synonyms.

Each word expresses a different kind of 保证.

- ✓ *Ensure* is more like 保障, 确保, meaning "to make sure something will or will not happen."
- ✓ *Assure* is more like 向 … 保证, and is often used to convince people (or pets, perhaps) not to worry.
- ✓ *Guarantee*, however, can do the work of both *ensure* and *assure*, depending on your preference.

Use *assure* to guarantee, to promise, to pledge, to convince. Use *ensure* to indicate things will (or will not) happen for certain.

Examples:

➢ 我保证我会第一个到场
I assure you that I will be the first to arrive.

Or

I guarantee I will be the first to arrive.

➢ 没有人能保证这项措施万无一失
No one can guarantee this measure is error-free.

➢ 谁能保证这项任务能按时完成？
Who can guarantee prompt completion of the task?

> 我向你保证, 你的事我一点都不知道。
> I can assure you that I know absolutely nothing about your story.

> 我保证孩子们一定喜欢这个地方。
> I assure you that children like this place.

> 要保证以后的一个星期, 家里有足够的食物和饮水。
> Three translations, each with different nuances:

1. You must make sure there is plenty of food and drinking water at home for next week.
   (You let people believe that you have food and water.)

2. You must assure/guarantee that there is plenty of food and drinking water at home for next week.
   (You pledge to people that you have food and water.)

3. You must make preparations to ensure plenty of food and drinking water are at home for next week.
   (The preparations guarantee plenty of food and water, not you.)

> 多准备几手方案能保证 (确保), 无论发生什么情况, 试验都能顺利进行。
> Multiple plans would ensure a smooth test, no matter what happens.
> (To say *plans assure that the test would be smooth* would suggest that plans can talk people into believing them.)

> 他们的出席保证了此项提案获得了多数票。
> Their presence ensured a majority vote on the bill.

> 你们要尽一切可能将救灾物资送到震灾人民手中。

You must do all you can to ensure relief supplies get into the hands of the earthquake victims.

被动 (bei dong): *passive* or *reactive*

I bet the first English word for 被动 that comes to mind is *passive*. That is true. The first time one translates 被动 as *passive* must be in English grammar classes, where passive voice renders 被动语态; hence, *passive* is earmarked for 被动.

However, in everyday conversation other than in English grammar class, *passive* carries a negative connotation: unwillingness to take actions, no desire to do things. Its synonyms include *inert*, *submissive*, *inactive*, *sluggish*, *involuntary*—more like its Chinese cousins 消极, 无为, 惰性.

But *reactive* is more like what 被动 is trying to say.

Simply put, *passive* means inaction; *reactive* means action in response to an action.

Passive is a choice not to act; its opposite is *active* 积极. *Reactive* is a choice not to act first but to act in response to an earlier action. Its opposite is *proactive* 主动.

The World Health Organization uses *passive* in the following statement: "The process of breathing secondhand smoke is called involuntary smoking or passive smoking."

Merriam-Webster's Dictionary has this example for *reactive*: "The government's response to the problem was *reactive* rather than proactive."

被动can appear in both cases above: 被动吸烟; 政府的被动反应. But *passive smoking* (被动吸烟) captures the involuntary nature of the action: I don't want to breathe in the cigarette smoke; whereas *reactive*, in the case of government response (政府的被动反应),

captures the action only as a response: the government acts but not proactively.

So the same 被动 renders both *passive* and *reactive* and perhaps something else.

Examples:

➤ 不做好准备, 谈判时就会陷入被动。
Without thorough preparation, a person might have to make only reactive moves during a negotiation.

➤ 你们应该主动问他, 不能被动地等他告诉你们。
You should go and ask him, instead of waiting for him to tell you.

➤ 客人都来了, 我们还不知道, 结果显得很被动。
We didn't know the guests were already here, so we were caught completely off guard.

➤ 我们应该主动, 不应被动。
We should be proactive, not reactive.

➤ 你们应该尽快设法摆脱被动局面。
You should try to get out of this unfavorable situation as soon as possible.

➤ 由于不了解市民的要求, 政府的调解工作很被动。
Because the government failed to understand what the residents wanted, its mediating efforts were ineffective.

➤ 我越挣扎, 绑匪越打我, 所以我就一动不动。
The more I struggled, the harder the kidnapper would hit me, so I became passive.

➤ 要力争扭转低价出口原材料的被动局面。
Efforts must be made to change the unfavorable situation of exporting raw materials at a low price.

➤ 局长秘书因收受贿赂被捕, 此案令局长十分被动。
The arrest of the bureau chief's secretary on charges of taking bribes makes the chief look very bad.

C

差别 (cha bie): *difference, disparity,* or *contrast*

These three words are all in the big family of 差别, but each has a different personality.

- ✓ *Difference* expresses a general concept of diversity, more like its Chinese cousin 不同.
- ✓ *Disparity* expresses the concept of inequality and unfair distribution involving moral judgment, more like its Chinese cousin 差距, 差异.
- ✓ *Contrast* expresses the concept of distinction, more like its Chinese cousin 反差; 对比.

Examples:

➤ 猎人要尽量减少自身伪装与背景的差别 (反差)
Hunters should minimize the contrast between their camouflage and the background.

(Camouflage and background are different things; but the idea is not to make camouflage stand out, hence the use of *contrast*, not *difference*.)

➤ 目前, 社会上的贫富差别还很大。
At present, the disparity (gap) between the rich and the poor is still very large.
(The difference in wealth is not a natural occurrence; rather, it is a result of social, systemic, or political factors.)

➤ 把红颜色放在白的旁边, 差别就看出来了!
Put the color red next to white, and you will see the contrast!

➤ 比一比这两幅画的画法, 你就看出差别了。
Compare the genres of these two paintings, and you will see the difference.

出发 (chu fa): *start* or not

This is not the one we use to mean *get going, let's go,* and the like. It often appears in this structure: 从 … 出发, as in 从整体利益出发; 从治病救人的角度出发, and many more such 出发 expressions.

Often, *starting from* is used to incorrectly translate 出发 in this context, leading readers to expect a sequence of actions.

But this 出发 is not about "start to do things"; rather, it is about how you look at things. It is a perspective, more like *taking something into consideration.*

Examples:

➤ 我们什么时候出发?
   When do we leave?

➤ 我们要从我国实际出发, 先进口设备, 然后自行研发。
   In light of China's actual conditions, we should import equipment first and later develop it on our own.

➤ 我们应从产品市场出发, 对整个市场走势做出分析。
   We should analyze the trend of the entire market by looking first at how the products are doing in the market.

➤ 我们应该从爱的角度出发, 耐心地帮助他。
   Out of love, we should help him with patience.

➤ 我们要从实际出发, 有多大本事, 就干多大事。。
   We should be realistic and only do what we are capable of doing.

➤ 我们要从全局出发, 不能只考虑自己。
   We must keep in mind the larger picture and not be preoccupied only with our own interests.

➤ 制定计划时, 我们要从长远利益出发, 把眼光放远一点。
   When making plans, we must take into account long-term interest and look far into the future.

➤ 我们应该从两国的利益出发, 以务实的态度处理这个问题。
   We should address this issue in a realistic manner from the perspective of the interests of the two nations.

出发点 (chu fa dian): *starting point* or not

出发点 can be translated as *starting point* or *point of departure* only when it means a physical (or mental) point from which people start to do something.

So "starting point" or "point of departure" is more about *beginning*—a *kickoff, first step, commencement*; more like 起点, 开始, 开端.

But in other cases, 出发点 means something totally different; rather, it means *intention, goal, objective, intent, aim, purpose*, and the like, more in line with 愿望, 本意, 动机. So 你的出发点是善良的 should be "Your intention is good," not "Your starting point is good."

Examples:

➤ 爸爸所有的出发点都是对儿子好, 可是, 他的溺爱最终还是把儿子毁了。
With all his good intentions, the father spoiled his son and eventually ruined him.

➤ 我的出发点是想帮他认识到问题的严重性。
My intention was to help him realize the seriousness of the problem.

➤ 爱的出发点不一定是身体, 但爱到了身体就到了顶点。(徐志摩)
Love may not necessarily intend to be physical love, but when it becomes physical, love reaches its climax. (*Xu Zhimo*)

➤ 这一款车以省油为出发点
The goal of this car is to save gas.

➤ 作者以大象的感情为出发点, 连续写出了一系列大象的分类, 大象的群体意识, 大象的保护等科普读物。

With the intent of writing about elephants' feelings, the author wrote a series of popular science books about elephant classification, elephant sense of group, and elephant protection, among others.

➤ 培养孩子们强烈的责任心是教育的出发点, 也是最终的归属. (four versions)

1. Installing a great sense of responsibility in our children is what education is all about.
2. The purpose of our education should be developing a great sense of responsibility in our children.
3. The ultimate goal of our education is to help our children develop a great sense of responsibility.
4. Ensuring that our children acquire a great sense of responsibility is at once the intent and ultimate goal of education.

➤ 我们所做的一切都应以国家利益为出发点 (four versions)

1. All we are doing must be based on national interest.
2. All we are doing must serve the interest of the nation.
3. All we are doing must revolve around national interest.
4. National interest must dictate what we are doing.

处理 (chu li): *process, treat* or not

In information technology, 处理 is often readily thought of as *processing,* as in *information processing* (信息处理), but not every 处理 has to be translated as *processing*. In everyday, nontechnical contexts, 处理 has a variety of renditions.

Examples:

➢ 内部装修前, 先要做结构处理。
Before home remodeling, one must treat the structure first.

➢ 这个问题如果处理不好, 会影响两家的关系。
If this problem is not handled properly, the good terms of the two families will be jeopardized.

➢ 这些苹果处理喽!
These apples are on sale!

➢ 把家里没有用的东西都处理掉。
Get rid of those things that we no longer need in the house.

➢ 总裁每天都要处理很多文件。
The president has to read a large number of documents each day.

➢ 秘书每天都要处理很多文件。
The secretary has to go over large piles of documents each day.

➢ 废物处理必须遵守环保政策。
Waste treatment has to follow environmental protection policies.

➢ 我真不知道该怎么处理跟他的关系。
I really don't know how to handle my relationship with him.

错过 (cuo guo): *miss* or *miss out on*

In a boxing match, we often hear commentators say, "Oh, he missed the punch!" In a shooting game, "He missed the target." In a singing practice, "He doesn't miss a beat." In explaining why he is late, "I missed the flight."

But in other cases, one must decide whether 错过 suggests the idea of "failure to do something," or whether it is actually saying, 可惜, 没赶上 (missed the fun; it is a regret).

For example, in 我错过了那次迎新会, the 错过 clearly suggests it is a party the person really wants to attend. So this 错过 needs *miss out on* to do the trick: *I missed out on the welcome party.* To say *I missed the welcome party* would mean only that you didn't come to the party, but it doesn't suggest you regret missing the fun.

Examples:

➤ 我错过了八点的那班车, 只好坐出租来办公室了
I missed the eight o'clock bus, so I had to take a cab to the office.
(Neither "do something" nor "enjoy" is suggested in the message.)

➤ 贷款利率下降了, 千万别错过机会!
The mortgage rate is coming down. Don't miss out on the opportunity!
(You want to be part of this opportunity.)

➤ 别错过练习!
Don't miss the practice!
(Come to the practice session.)

Don't miss out on the practice!
(Come to the practice session. It is a lot of fun.)

➤ 对不起, 我错过了吃冰淇淋这么好的事。
I am sorry I missed out on the ice cream.

(To say *I missed the ice cream* would mean something else: you failed to catch the ice cream tossed at you. It doesn't have the sense of *enjoy the ice cream*.)

➤ 我不想错过这个机会
I don't want to miss the opportunity.
(It simply suggests that you would do what the opportunity calls for you to do—accepting an offer, taking on a low-interest loan, and the like.)

I don't want to miss out on the opportunity.
(The word *opportunity* clearly suggests something fun, something you would do as a member of a group.)

➤ 不要错过生活中美好的东西!
Don't miss out on life!
(To say *don't miss life* would translate as 不要怀念/想念生活.)

➤ 你错过了好多好玩的事!
You have missed out on a lot!
(To say you *have missed a lot* would mean simply 错过了好多, and what had been missed might not necessarily be 好玩的事; most likely, it translates as 你有很多没听懂, or 没赶上, or 没看见.)

D

单位 /工作单位 (dan wei): *work unit* or not

单位 refers to a workplace or employer, but it is often translated as *work unit*. Not terribly wrong, but often, one has to be in the context of China in order for *work unit* to mean 单位.

In the English-language world, terms such as *workplace, employer, office, company, agency,* and so forth are often used instead.

The term *work unit*, on the other hand, could mean a unit of measurement for work, part of a larger family of measurement units: energy unit (joule, calorie, kWh, etc.), heat unit (joule, SI, BTU, watt, etc.), currency unit (dollar, euro, yuan, etc.), weight unit (ton, kilogram, pound, etc.), and measurement unit (mm, cm, m, km, g, kg, l, ml, etc.).

So, to follow this logic, *work unit* could mean a unit that measures your work, though that's a bit stretch—pieces assembled per hour, parts produced per day, time used for completing a project, and the like.

Furthermore, in the English-language world, *unit* is often used to refer to a department, an office, or a branch of an organization—the Chinese term of 部门 of a 工作单位, as in, "He works in the audio-visual unit of the library."

So the temptation of translating 单位 to *work unit* does a disservice to the term, especially when the reader is not familiar with this one-size-fits-all Chinese expression for company, office, employer, at work, workplace, and so forth.

Examples:

➢ 我在单位不能上网。
I don't have Internet access at work.

➤ 我们单位领导不准我的假。

My supervisor didn't approve my leave request.

➤ 哦, 他是我们单位的一个熟人。

Oh, he is someone I know at work.

➤ 明天我开单位的车去接你。

I will drive the company car to pick you up tomorrow.

➤ 你们单位是不是在那个楼?

Is your office in that building?

➤ 我们在单位不能上网干私事。

We are not allowed to go online for personal things at the workplace.

➤ 你是哪个单位的?

Where do you work?

Or

Who is your employer?

➤ 优厚的待遇使这家公司名列去年100家最佳工作单位榜首。

The generous perks helped land the company at the top of our list of the 100 best wokplaces last year.

Note: The political culture is behind rendering 单位 (工作单位) as *work unit*, instead of *employer*, often by native Chinese speakers. The English term *employer* does not sound as politically correct to the Chinese, who are so accustomed to thinking in terms of equalitarianism.

The word *employer* carries the notion of 雇主, 资本家 and, by extension, 剥削 (exploitation), something that Mao and his followers have fought hard to eradicate from the face of China, whereas *work* is associated with 工作, 劳动, a concept much glorified by the political culture and therefore politically correct.

道德 (dao de): *moral (morality)* or *ethical (ethics)*

道德 has two English cousins: *morals* and *ethics,* both referring to principles whereby one makes a judgment of what is right or wrong. But they are not absolute synonyms, each referring to a different category of 道德.

Simply put, use *moral (morality)* when 道德 refers to judgment of a good or bad person; use *ethical (ethics)* when 道德 refers to judgment of right or wrong things.

In other words, *moral (morality)* is about personal character; *ethical (ethics)* is about professional conduct. *Morality* is a value system governing one's personal life; *ethics* is the code of conduct established by a profession. Being *ethical* is about being a good employee; being *moral* is about being a good person.

So a mail carrier may find abortion immoral, and it is morally wrong to have anything personally to do with abortion clinics, but it is ethically right to deliver mail to abortion clinics and do it with all due professionalism.

When 道德 is used in the context of, say, a company's code of conduct, translate 道德 as *ethics* (or *ethical*), as in 职业道德培训 (*ethics training*). When道德 is used in the context of a person's morality, translate 道德 as *morality* (or *moral*), as in 她有她的道德标准. (*She has her moral standards.*)

The phrase below can be translated three ways, each carrying a different meaning of 道德:

➤ 这样做不道德

This is not ethical.

(Scenario: someone takes office supplies home.)

Or

This is immoral.

(Scenario: someone mistreats children.)

Or

This is both immoral and unethical.

(Scenario: someone cheats on a company test. This person violates both his personal moral standards and the company code of conduct.)

等 (deng): *etc.* or not

等 has two functions: (1) as *etc.*; and(2) as an *end marker of a list of things.*

As an *end marker* of a list of things, 等does not need to be translated. It serves as no more or less than a period.

Examples: as an *end marker*

➤ 客人们参观了北京, 天津, 上海, 杭州等四座城市。

The guests visited four cities: Beijing, Tianjin, Shanghai, and Hangzhou.

➤ 长江, 黄河, 黑龙江, 海河, 珠江等五大河流是我们今天要讨论的重点。

The Yangtze River, the Yellow River, the Heilongjiang River, the Haihe River, and the Pearl River are the focus of our discussion today.

Examples: as *etc.*:

➤ 法国, 日本等国都纷纷将汽车市场扩展到中国。
France and Japan, among many others, have all expanded their car markets into China.

➤ 我们购买了桌子和椅子等办公室用具。
We have purchased desks, chairs, and other office equipment.
Or
We have purchased, among other office supplies, desks and chairs.

➤ 布什总统在上海吃了扬州炒饭, 上海小笼包等.
While in Shanghai, President Bush tried Yangzhou fried rice, Shanghai steamed dumplings, and other local dishes.

定位 (ding wei): *positioning* or *locating*

定位 is often used in technical documents, such as in 导航定位, 卫星定位 to mean a position with a reference point in a geographic area or the coordinate system.

But is it *positioning* or *locating* every time we come across 定位? There are real-time locating systems (RTLS) to identify and track the location of objects in real time, but they are also referred to as being a form of a local positioning system.

So here we are: a locating system and a positioning system, both rendered as 定位系统 in Chinese. When do we use *locating,* and when do we use *positioning*?

Granted, both *locating* and *positioning*, in everyday usage, mean finding where an object is, and, for an accurate location, they both express where an object is in terms of latitude and longitude.

21

But there is a subtle difference. While *locating* yields the location of an object relative to what the object is close to (namely, near the door, at the bottom of the lake, and so forth), *positioning* detects the location of an object with a reference point in the coordinate system (namely, its latitude and longitude from, say, a satellite perspective).

To exaggerate the difference a bit, *locating* may be used to suggest a general geographic location and *positioning* a coordinate system, although in many cases they can be used interchangeably.

So we have three 定位系统 here. While both 全球定位系统 (global positioning system) and 个人定位系统 (personal positioning system) use *positioning*, 人员定位系统 personnel locator system uses *locator* (thus, *locating*).

The first system (全球定位系统) may be a satellite-based system, working on the latitude and longitude.

The second system (个人定位系统) may be a person-carried system to respond to the satellite-based GPS; both work to provide a location in terms of coordinates.

The third system (人员定位系统) is meant to tell where someone is, say, deep in a coal mine. It may not need the coordinates to locate a person.

The same is true for 水下定位信标 (underwater locator beacon), where, again, *locator* (*locating*) is used for 定位. Clearly, the system finds the location of an object by receiving signals, not coordinates, transmitted from the object.

There is another subtle distinction: *locating* may give a general location, whereas *positioning* may give a specific location.

对象 (dui xiang): *target* or *object*

A common translation for 对象 is *target*, but not all 对象 is *target*, especially when *target* appears in the context of attacking (military or personal), striking, ridicule, and the like.

There are other, better choices.

Examples:

➤ 在学校, 他常常是别人讥笑的对象。
He is often the target of ridicule at school.

➤ 他因用词不当, 一时成为公众的批判对象。
Because of his improper choice of words, he immediately became the target of public denunciation.

➤ 公安部门这一季度的打击对象是跨省贩毒。
The target for public security's campaign for this quarter is cross-province drug trafficking.
(The above three samples are meant to show that *target* is appropriate often in the context of ridicule, denunciation, or matters to that effect.)

➤ 培训对象来自各个国家。
Trainees are from various countries.

➤ 今天的采访对象是我们的老熟人。
The person we are interviewing today is our old acquaintance.

➤ 我们要明确我们的销售对象是谁。
We must be clear who our customers are.
(Translated into *sales targets*, it would be mistaken as 销售目标 *sales goals*.)

> ➤ 他们的研究对象是80后这一代人。
> The group of people they are studying is the generation born in the 1980s.

> ➤ 他是领导班子的发展对象。
> He is the potential candidate for future leadership.

> ➤ 我们爱的对象是我们的孩子。
> Our love is our children.

F

仿真 (fang zhen): *simulate* or *emulate*

Dictionaries have both of them for 仿真. They both mean "copy" all right, but they each "copy" in a different way.

Often, *simulate* means re-creation of a given situation to get the same results as a real one gives; *emulate* means to imitate the inner characteristics of something or someone.

In other words, one *simulates* the outer features but *emulates* inner qualities. *Simulation* is more about testing a scenario, finding out whether something works; *emulation* is more about mirroring a quality, hoping to be what is being imitated.

In computing, a simulator (such as a flight simulator) is software that duplicates various situations to test functionalities of, say, a system; an emulator is hardware that duplicates the functions of a real system to function like a real one.

So *simulate* is more like 仿真, 模拟; *emulate* is more like 模仿, 仿效.

Examples:

- 仿真结果表明, 机器人能在极端情况下, 完成搜索任务
  Simulation results show that robots can complete search tasks under extreme conditions.

- 计算机仿真现被广泛用于探究飓风形成的原因
  Computer simulation is now widely used to gain new insights into the formation of tornadoes.

- 许多实验目前都通过电脑模拟来完成
  Many tests are now done through computer simulation.

- 模仿家长, 是孩子成长的一部分
  Emulating their parents is part of children's growing up.

- 学生们效仿他们老师的风格
  Students emulated the style of their teachers.

- 为了让歌迷们兴奋起来, 歌手们模仿迈克 . 杰克逊的舞步
  To fire up the fans, the artists emulated Michael Jackson's dance moves.

- 委员会希望找到一个大家都能效仿的作法
  The committee is trying to find a practice that can be widely emulated.

- 人们希望通过效仿前辈的成功来实现他们的梦想
  People are trying to make their dreams come true by emulating the success of predecessors.

> ➤ 需要在另一台计算机上模仿跳频功能
> We need to emulate the frequency of hopping on another computer.

复杂 (fu za): *complex* or *complicated*

Most dictionaries use *complex* to explain *complicated* or the other way around, thus further reinforcing the impression that these two can be used synonymously.

A careful look into the context in which they are used, however, will show a clear pattern of difference in usage and meaning.

Complex indicates that something has many parts, often physical ones; mostly used to describe a structure, an organization, a construction layout, and the like. It is more a physical reality.

Complicated conveys the notion of judgment, a subjective view involving some degree of effort in understanding and explaining matters involved; mostly used to describe an idea, a plan, a concept, or a statement that requires effort to comprehend. It is more a mental reality.

A *complex* matter may not necessarily be *complicated*. A rocket scientist would not say a rocket is a complicated carrier, but my grandma may find it painfully complicated.

In other words, if you say, "This system is complex," others hear "The system includes numerous components." However, if you say, "It is a complicated system," others may hear "It takes some effort to understand and explain the ins and outs of the system."

Complex is about the numerous components, more like 复杂, often a statement of facts; *complicated* is about one's ability to figure out the intricacy of something, more like 棘手, 难懂, often a suggestion of some degree of frustration.

Therefore, *complicated* is often used, not without acknowledging some degree of frustration, to describe issues that require effort

26

to comprehend: a complicated process; a complicated story; a complicated issue; a complicated relationship; a complicated person; a complicated health care plan—or rather, a complex and complicated health care plan.

A good example of *complex* can be found in the description of Jefferson's Bible on the second floor of the Smithsonian National Museum of American History in Washington, DC. It reads, "Jefferson's book presented complex conservation problems. It contains twelve different types of paper, six printing inks, four manuscript inks, two adhesives, linen thread, silk thread, and goatskin leather."

Another example of *complex* is found on the Haagen-Dazs coffee ice cream container. It reads, "Our legendary coffee ice cream is crafted from the finest Brazilian coffee beans, specially roasted and brewed to bring out their rich, complex flavor."

A good example of *complicated* was on NPR news on April 12, which commented on there being three days to file your tax return. "The tax code," the news went on, "is full of complicated loopholes and deductions that require professional translation."

Examples:

> 人的脊椎是一个复杂的结构, 由三组称为 "椎骨" 的骨头组成
> The human spine is a complex structure of three groups of bones called "vertebrae."
> (*Complex*: lots of bones for sure but no suggestion of difficulties in understanding the intricacies.)

Or

> The human spine is a complicated structure of three groups of bones called "vertebrae."
> (*Complicated*: requires some effort to grasp the intricacies of human spine.)

➤ 这套系统很复杂

This system is complex.

(This system consists of lots of parts.)

Or

This system is complicated.

(It requires some effort to understand how the system operates.)

➤ 抚养孩子是个漫长, 复杂的过程。

Bringing up a child is a long, complex process.

(It requires lots of effort and a great variety of activities over many years.)

Or

Bringing up a child is a long, complicated process.

(Not only does it take many years, but it is difficult.)

➤ 有的东西很复杂, 但不难懂。

Something may be complex but not complicated.

➤ "你既然不喜欢他, 为什么不跟他分手呢? "

"Since you don't like him, why don't you break up with him?"

"咳! 一两句话说不清。"

"Well, it is complicated."

➤ 他的出现打乱了整个格局。

His presence has complicated the situation.

➤ 从此刻起, 日子就变得复杂了。

This is where life gets complicated.

(It is about difficulties and frustrations.)

> 这项计划具体执行起来很复杂

The logistics for this plan are complex.

(It involves many agencies, procedures, financing issues, etc.)

Or

The logistics for this plan are complicated.

(It is a difficult task.)

> 你把它搞得这么复杂干嘛？

Why are you making it so complicated?

(You are making it hard to understand.)

G

干扰 (gan rao): *interference* or *jamming*

干扰 becomes a translation issue only when used in a technological field, such as 信号干扰, 电磁干扰, not in a nontechnological sense, such as 干扰他的生活, 干扰会场, 干扰他国内部事务.

Dictionaries list both *interference* and *jamming* under 干扰 without any distinctions, but the two are not synonyms. There is a difference.

Simply put, *interference* is unintentional; *jamming* is a deliberate act to cause damage. In wartime, rivalries *jam* each other's communications systems.

In other words, *jamming* is interference, but *interference* is not always jamming, which can be disruption due to system malfunction.

So the context of the following sentences should tell whether 干扰 is *interference* or *jamming*.

> 近距离同时使用多个无线话筒会造成干扰
>
> Interference may occur when multiple wireless microphones are being used in close proximity.
>
> (Signal interruption is not intentional.)

> 早期无线电干扰方式是发送噪音干扰
>
> Early-stage radio jamming was done by noise jamming.
>
> (It is clearly a deliberate act to cause harm.)

> 在电子战中, 干扰机通过发送干扰信号阻断敌方雷达信号。
>
> In electric warfare, jammers emit jamming signals to block enemy radar signals.

根据 (gen ju): *according to* or *based on*

There is a subtle distinction between the two. While *according to* can easily find its Chinese cousin 按照, both *according to* and *based on* are often used indiscriminately to translate as 根据.

But they are not quite the same.

Simply put, *according to* often denotes that a piece of information is provided clearly, and one acts exactly as so instructed. For example:

✓ *According to you, even a caveman can do it.* (You said that a caveman could do it.)

✓ *The table was assembled according to the instructions.* (The instruction book shows specific steps of how to assemble the table.)

✓ *Kevin was appointed CEO according to the decision.* (The decision instructs that Kevin be appointed CEO.)

However, *based on* often denotes that a piece of information is used primarily as a reference for one's judgment, a point from which an opinion is developed. It may not tell one exactly what to do. For example:

- ✓ *Based on your theory, one can say that even a caveman can do it.* (You may not have said these words—*a caveman can do it*—but you suggested something to this effect.)
- ✓ *Kevin was appointed CEO based on the decision.* (The decision may have said, as a general principle, *those who have served the company for forty years are eligible for the position*, and the board of directors chose Kevin among many candidates because he met the requirement.)
- ✓ *We changed our troop deployment plans based on new enemy situations.* (The decision was made in light of recent enemy situations; the enemy didn't tell us what to do [*according to the enemy*].)

So one draws a conclusion from (根据) his/her own reasoning.

Examples:

➢ 根据董事会指示, Tom 被任命为经理。
According to the board of directors' instructions, Tom is appointed the manager.
(The instructions may say, "Appoint Tom the general manager.")
Or
Based on the board of directors' instructions, Tom is appointed the manager.
(The instructions may say, "Appoint the qualified one the general manager.")

31

➢ 根据天气预报，明天不便外出野餐。

According to the weather forecast, tomorrow is not a good day for a picnic.

(The weather report says that people should not plan picnics tomorrow because of possible heavy rainstorms.)

Or

Based on the weather forecast, tomorrow is not a good day for a picnic.

(We decided not to have the picnic because the weather report says there will be heavy rainstorms tomorrow.)

➢ 根据计划，我们派 Jane 到现场。

According to the plan, we will send Jane to the site.

(The plan says, "Send Jane to the site.")

Or

Based on the plan, we will send Jane to the site.

(The plan says that we should send a technician to the site. Jane is a technician.)

➢ 我们根据敌情，把部队分散在东西两侧。

According to the enemy situation, we will position our troops on the east and west flanks.

(The enemy situation reveals a favorable window of opportunity.)

Or

Based on the enemy situation, we will position our troops on the east and west flanks.

(We studied the enemy situation and decided to position our troops as such.)

➢ 我们根据客户的意见，决定周日继续办公。

Based on customer feedback, we decided to open on the weekend.

(Customers may say that they have time only on weekends, but they may not specifically suggest we work on Sundays. It is our decision.)

Or

According to customer feedback, we decided to continue to work on the weekend.

(Customers may suggest specifically that we open on Sundays.)

Let's change the perspectives and see how *according to* and *based on* are used in English expressions, without involving translation, just to get a feel for the difference between the two.

➤ According to the instructions, the doorknob should be put on first.
➤ According to the directions, the paint should be applied twice.
➤ Discrimination based on race, gender, and religion is unlawful.
➤ The movie is based on a true story.
➤ Promotion based on job performance is a common practice in the industry.

Again, let's take a look at the following *according to* expressions cited in *Collins English Dictionary & Treasures* and *Oxford Advanced Learner's Dictionary.*

➤ They both played the game according to the rules.
➤ If all goes according to plan, the first concert will be Tuesday evening.
➤ You've been absent six times, according to our record.
➤ According to local gossip, Philip and his father haven't been in touch for years.
➤ Prices vary according to the quantity ordered.
➤ The salary will be fixed according to qualifications and experience.

Note: In some cases, *according to* and *based on* may mean roughly the same. It is only when a distinction must be made that one needs to use them separately.

功能 (gong neng): *function* or *functionality*

They are both listed under 功能, but they mean different things. While *function* suggests tasks to be performed, *functionality* emphasizes the ability to perform those tasks.

But, be careful. *Functionality* is not a fancy version of *function*, nor does it make you sound more professional. The two simply say two different things.

Function is about particular roles; *functionality* is about abilities.

Examples:

➤ 这套系统需要定义一个软件功能，也就是该系统能提供的功能及服务。

This system needs to define a software function, namely its functionalities and services.

(The first 功能 clearly refers to a role/task, with the help of 一个, a measure word, and the second 功能 refers to the system's abilities to perform certain functions.)

➤ 产品功能介绍

Product functions

(If 功能 refers to specific functions/roles/tasks)

Or

Product functionalities

(If 功能 refers to abilities to perform these functions)

> 此项新应用程序有以下功能

This new application has the following functionalities.

(If 功能 refers to abilities)

Or

This new application performs the following functions.

(If 功能 refers to specific functions/roles/tasks)

> 功能齐全

A complete set of functions

(If 功能 refers to specific functions/roles/tasks)

Or

A complete set of functionalities

(If 功能 refers to abilities)

> 用手机搜索功能可以找到目标, 因为手机有这个功能。

One can use a cell phone's "Search" function to find targets, because cell phones have this functionality.

(The first 功能 clearly refers to a searching task; the second 功能 refers to its ability.)

Or

One can use a cell phone's "Search" function to find targets, because cell phones have this function.

(The first 功能 clearly refers to a specific task; the second 功能 repeats the same task.)

关系 (guan xi): *relation, relationship,* or *connection*

In many cases, *relation* and *relationship* can be loosely used as a near synonym—the relationship/relation between the two files. It is especially so, generally, when used to refer to technical subjects.

In some cases, however, when human factors are involved, *relationship* will part with *relation* to take on a different meaning all to itself: intimacy.

Relation is more about contacts, ties, and association; namely, in what capacity one is related to the other—blood relation, labor relation, public relations, race relation, international relations, industrial relations, diplomatic relations—or in what capacity one is connected in relation to the other, such as parents and children, players and coach, coworkers, next-door neighbors, and so forth.

Relationship, on the other hand, is more about the quality of the relation; namely, how the relation is developing: a good relationship with my sister, a close relationship with my children, a bumpy relationship between the two countries.

Simply put, *relation* is about *who* and *what*; relationship is about *how*. *Relation* is described in terms of *what* and *relationship* in terms of *how*.

We change a *relation,* but we strengthen a *relationship.*

A marriage counselor gives *relationship* (love, intimacy) advice, rather than *relation* (boyfriend-and-girlfriend) advice.

When one asks, "What is your relation to her?" the response may be, "She is my sister."

When one asks: "How is your relationship with her?" the response may be, "We are very close."

When one says, "Yes, I am Ted Roosevelt, not related to President Roosevelt," he is saying he is not related by blood to the president.

When one says, "I have always had a difficult *relationship* with my brother," he is saying they are not close to each other, but he is blood-related to his brother nonetheless.

When we see a newspaper headline, "Middletown Small Business Conference Strengthens Relationships in a Growing Market," we read, the conference helps facilitate cooperation among small businesses.

When we say *public relations*, we are talking about a connection, you *vs.* others, the sheer effort to reach out to the public. If an organization has a good image, it will enjoy a good *relationship* with its public. The Public Relations Society of America (PRSA) states that "public relations" is a process that builds mutually beneficial relationships between organizations and their public.

When we say *relation* between smoking and heart disease, we are talking about relevance of nicotine in your body to your heart condition. It is about connection.

When we say *labor relations*, we are talking about contact between management and workers. So, proper management of labor relations often results in positive relationships between management and workers.

When a pastor says: *What matters most is your relationship with God*, he is talking about how close you are to God, not who is who (*relation*) in the grand scheme of God's creation.

He first stated that he had no sexual *relations* (contact) with her, only to admit days later that his *relationship* (romance) with her was inappropriate. The former suggests capacity in which the two were involved; the latter indicates intimacy.

中美关系 may have two renditions: *Sino-US relations* and a *Sino-US relationship* both are often used to mean the same thing, generally speaking. But in certain cases, the former (*relations*) may refer to contacts, such as in trade or diplomatic, economic, academic, and military. It is about in which capacities the two countries interact. The latter (*relationship*) refers to how the two countries are getting along in those capacities, good or bad.

Two countries establish diplomatic relations; namely, ties, contacts. They enjoy close relationships; namely, friendship, cooperation.

As for other 关系, there are many ways to translate, depending on the context.

Examples:

➤ 两国的贸易关系不断发展, 文化交流日益增加。

The two countries are seeing a constant development in trade relations and a steady rise in cultural exchanges.

➤ 我们两家的关系很近。

Our two families are very close.

➤ 他的关系多, 让他办准行。

He knows a lot of people there. I am sure it will get done if you let him do it.

➤ 看来我非得用我的关系不可了。

It looks like I have to use my connections.

➤ 现在办什么事都得靠关系。

One needs connections for everything.

➤ 这个决定关系到公司的前途, 你要三思。

This decision is about the company's future; you must think twice.

➤ 这件事关系重大, 不容迟缓, 得立即告诉她的家人。

This is a significantly important matter and should not wait another minute. We must notify her family immediately.

➤ 这个决定关系重大, 必须由董事会通过。

With a lot at stake, this decision must be cleared by the board of directors.

> 研究结果表明, 妇女更注意社会团体中和婚姻感情中的细微表现。
> Research findings show that women are more attuned to the intricacies of social groups and relationships.

Note: *relation* and *relationship* in science and technology are a different story. They are often used interchangeably.

规定 (gui ding): *regulation* or not

规定, both as a noun and a verb, is one of those Chinese expressions used in all kinds of documents. Depending on context, it can be rendered more than just *regulation*.

As a noun, it is often translated as *regulation*, but as a verb, it is often *lay down, lay out, stipulate, specify, list, outline*, and so forth.

Examples:

> 按照有关部门规定, 出口产品要有出口许可。
> According to regulations by the authorities, one must have a permit to do export business.

> 除了携带规定的物品外, 登山人员还带了少量的药品。
> In addition to the required items, the climbers also brought a small amount of medicines.

> 校方规定, 毕业生一律参加一个月的社区服务活动。
> The school ruled that all graduating students must spend one month in community service.

➤ 我们要在规定的时间内完成这个项目。

We must finish this project in the timeframe prescribed.

➤ 这项政策规定, 年满60岁的人可享受免费医疗。

This policy stipulates that people sixty years of age may enjoy free medical treatment.

➤ 合同上规定了此项试验的条件。

The contract specifies the conditions for the test.

➤ 我们应该按照说明书上规定的步骤一步一步地做。

We should do it step by step, following the procedures outlined in the instructions.

国家 (guo jia): *country, nation,* or *state*

In many cases, *country* and *nation* can be used interchangeably. An EU official may refer to EU members as *countries* one moment and *nations* the next, all in one breath. We may also say, *There are around two hundred countries in the world.*

"I'll serve this great country for years" ran the headline of the *Sun* (UK) on the occasion of Queen Elizabeth's Diamond Jubilee. But immediately following this headline, it read, "The Queen yesterday rededicated herself to the nation in a speech to Parliament to celebrate her Diamond Jubilee."

In some cases, for a clearer presentation a distinction is desired.

Country is often used relative to the people living in that country. One may say, *I love my country* (seldom *I love my nation*), in appreciation of the land and the people, not in relation to other countries. Lin Yutang (林语堂), the renowned Chinese scholar, gave his book 吾国吾民 the title, *My Country, My People*, to suggest the sense of "people" in the word *country*.

Nation, on the other hand, is often used to suggest the sense of "sovereignty," relative to other nations. We have the League of Nations and the United Nations, not the "United Countries," in the sense that each nation is a sovereign member.

We say *national anthem* in relation to other countries, meaning each country has its own anthem (*national* could also be thought of as the adjective form of *country*). We may say *build a strong country*, when we have us, the citizens of the country, in mind. We may say *build a strong nation*, when we have other nations in mind, from the standpoint of the world as a whole.

In his 2012 inaugural address, Russia's president Putin used *country* and *nation* in one breath, as follows: "We have strengthened our country and returned our dignity as a great nation." He went on to say, "We must all understand that the life of our future generations and our prospects as a country and nation depend on us today …" He is obviously speaking to his people when he uses *country* and to the world when he uses *nation*.

State, on the other hand, is a different story. It is more about government function, among other distinctions. We say *state-run business*, not *nation-run* or *country-run business*. We say a *nuclear-weapon state*, more in the sense that it is the government business to develop nuclear weapons, not the choice of its people.

We say *head of state* for 国家首脑, not *head of nation* or *head of country*, to mean more about government function.

Examples:

➢ 国事访问
State visit

➢ 国家企业
State-owned enterprise

➢ 出席国宴的嘉宾
State-dinner guests

➢ 国家利益与外交手段的关系
Relationship between national interest and diplomatic maneuvers
(How closely the two work together)

➢ 国家派出的工程人员
Engineers sent by the government

➢ 国家资助的项目
Government-sponsored project
Or
State-funded project

➢ 意大利海军格言: 国家, 荣誉
Italian Navy motto: Country and Honor

➢ 挪威皇家空军格言: 为了国王和国家
Royal Norwegian Air Force motto: For King and Country

➢ 国家规定, 省级干部一年只能出国三次。
The central government policy is that provincial-level officials are allowed only three overseas trips a year.

➢ 国家要用几年的时间建成一个自由贸易区。
It takes a few years for the state to build a free trade zone.

➤ 法国人从本杰明•富兰克林身上看到了这个新兴的
美洲国家。

The French people saw, through Benjamin Franklin, the new American nation.

➤ 有核国家

Nuclear state

(Developing nuclear weapons is more a government policy than its people's choice; thus, *state*.)

H

和 (he): *and* or *as well as*

It is not about 和 being translated as *and*. They are a good match. The problem is when 和 is translated to *as well as*.

And and *as well as* are not the same. In fact, *and* is 和. It conjoins elements equal in significance, much the same as what 和 does; but *as well as* is not 和. Not at all. It conjoins unequal parts, meaning *in addition to* …

Again, let me repeat, never, never, never use *as well as* to translate 和!

Examples:

➤ 他请了他以前的同事和一些新朋友

He invited his former coworkers and his new friends.

(His former coworkers and new friends are given equal attention.)

Or

He invited his former coworkers as well as his new friends.

(He *not only* invited his new friends, but he also invited his former coworkers. Special attention is given to the coworkers.)

➤ 我买了一辆新车和两个婴儿安全座椅

I bought a new car and two infant car seats.

(The new car and car seats are treated equally.)

Or

I bought a new car as well as two infant car seats.

(I not only bought two car seats but also a new car, with more interest shown in the new car.)

➤ 国际奥委会访问了荷兰, 比利时, 日本和德国。

IOC visited Holland, Belgium, Japan, and Germany.

(The four countries are treated equally.)

Or

IOC visited Holland, Belgium, and Japan, as well as Germany.

(IOC visited *not only* Germany but also the other three countries, with emphasis on these three countries.)

Often, in simple conjunction sentences, people do not translate 和 as *as well as*, as in 苹果和梨都好, 他和我都来, 今天和明天都冷, 美国和日本我都喜欢, and the like. In these simple conjunctions, *and* is sufficient for 和.

But two temptations are the cause of the mistranslation of 和 as *as well as*.

Temptation 1: avoid repeated use of *and* for 和

➤ 公司非常重视员工培训, 项目研发, 和人才留用。

The company is giving great importance to staff training, research and development, and retaining talent.

(With *and*, the three elements are connected as equal effort.)

Or

The company is giving great importance to staff training, research and development, as well as retaining talent.

(The use of *as well as* is an attempt to avoid a second *and*, only to twist the meaning a bit to read "Just as it takes effort to retain talent, the company makes an effort in staff training and R&D.")

Temptation 2: match *as well as* with 以及, assuming *as well as* is a formal version of *and*, much like 以及 of 和. But the meaning is twisted.

Unlike 和, 以及 often conjoins a long list of objects. Perhaps the rationale behind the 以及 usage is this: after a long list of items, one needs a conjunction "heavier" than a single word 和 to balance the weight, with an extra word. For example:

➤ 川菜, 鲁菜, 淮菜, 粤菜, 闽菜, 浙菜, 湘菜, 以及徽菜构成了中国的八大菜系。

The eight major Chinese cuisines include Sichuan cuisine, Shandong cuisine, Jiangsu cuisine, Guangdong cuisine, Yunnan cuisine, Zhejiang cuisine, *as well as* Anhui cuisine.

(It is an incorrect translation. The eight cuisines are equal parts, no one being superior to the other. Therefore, use of a simple *and* serves the purpose beautifully.)

Using *as well as* in the above translation twists the meaning. It suggests that *not only* is Anhui cuisine part of Chinese cuisine but that the first seven cuisines are also Chinese cuisine, as if one was trying to say the first seven cuisines were as famous as Anhui cuisine.

Let's look at a *New York Times* article where *as well as* is used, *not* to mean *and*:

"Lasers are not effective in bad weather because the beam can be disturbed or scattered by water vapor, as well as by smoke, sand, and dust."[2]

If *as well as* is translated back to 和, then it suggesting that *smoke, sand,* and *dust* are part of *bad weather*. Clearly, it is not the case. The passage is saying that water vapor affects lasers *as much as* smoke, sand, and dust do.

合法 (he fa): *legal* or *lawful* or *legitimate*

Legal is about the way one applies law—what the procedures tell one to do. *Lawful* suggests the substance of law—what the law tells one to do or not to do.

Legal is more about *how* one approaches a matter allowed by law. It involves rules, regulations, and formalities. *Lawful* is more about *what* is permitted by law.

Laws are made by lawmakers; legalities are created by lawyers.

In other words, when *legal* is followed by an action, it suggests the action follows the required procedures. When *lawful* is followed by an action, it suggests the action is allowed by law.

Therefore, *legal entry into the country* means a person enters the country with proper documents, such a passport or visa. *Lawful entry into the country* suggests the person is allowed by certain provisions in the law to enter the country.

But when *legal* and *lawful* are each followed by a noun, they often mean the same thing: it is allowed by law. Therefore, in the *Washington Post* (July 11, 2013), *unlawful gifts* and *illegal gifts*

---

[2] http://www.nytimes.com/2013/04/09/

are used interchangeably in a story about censuring DC Council member Marion Barry for accepting gifts from city contractors.

Legitimate is something people perceive as legal, lawful, or simply acceptable. It's Chinese version is 合理.

Examples:

➢ 要想在美国取得合法身份, 必须以合法途径进入美国。
One must enter the United States legally if he/she wishes to apply for a lawful status in the United States.

➢ 合法婚姻的法律定义
Legal definitions for a lawful marriage

➢ 继承法规定, 长子是家族企业的合法继承人。
According to inheritance law, the oldest son of the family is the lawful heir to the family enterprise.

➢ 网络营销是合法生意。公司是注册的, 并且是上市公司。
Network marketing is a legitimate business. The company is registered and publicly traded.
(The public accepts it.)

➢ 这些合理要求必须通过合法程序递交到有关部门。
These legitimate requests must be submitted to appropriate agencies through legal procedures.

➢ 在这个边远的村子里, 一旦举办了婚宴, 一桩婚姻就算
是合法的。

In this remote village, a marriage is deemed legitimate once a wedding banquet is thrown for the villagers.

(*Legitimate marriage*: villagers accept the husband-and-wife status. *Legal marriage*: the couple files legal/government-issued papers.)

➢ 这个手续不合法

This procedure is not legal.

(It does not follow steps allowed by law.)

➢ 注册公司要通过合法程序

Registering a company must follow legal procedures.

➢ 在美国, 人们必须通过合法手段获取隐蔽携带枪支的许可证,
以备合法自卫之用。

In the US, a license to carry a concealed weapon for lawful self-defense must be obtained through legal means.

➢ 当车子合法地停在一个地方或合法地停下时, 人们仍然可以
发送短信。

One can still send text messages in the car when it is lawfully parked or lawfully stopped.

合理 (he li): *rational* or *reasonable*

Again, dictionaries list *rational* and *reasonable* for 合理 but fail to say there is a difference between the two.

While *rational* emphasizes a judgment based on reason rather than emotions, *reasonable* suggests judgment acceptable to normal practice.

So *rational* is more in line with 理智, 理性, 明智, 冷静; its synonym is *logic*. *Reasonable* is more about 合理, 合情, 公道; its synonyms are *sound, fair*.

Below is how *rational* and *reasonable* are cited in English dictionaries and how they should be rendered in Chinese. The difference is clear.

➤ I can't be rational when so many things are happening at the same time!
这么多事同时发生, 你让我怎么冷静!

➤ She argued her case calmly and rationally.
她沉着冷静地陈述她的理由。

➤ This is no rational explanation for his behavior.
他的所作所为不可理喻。

➤ No rational person would ever behave like that.
一个理智的人是不会这样做的。

➤ The patient appeared perfectly rational.
那个病人看上去头脑非常清醒。

➤ Is it rational to believe that there are alien beings from outer space?
相信有外星人的想法说得通吗?

➤ This is a more reasonable price.
这个价钱还比较合理。

➤ He made a reasonable offer for the car.
他的这个车的价格还算合理。

➢ You must submit your claim within a reasonable time.
你必须在适当的时间内递交你的索赔表。

➢ Be reasonable! We can't work late every night。
讲点道理好不好! 我们不能天天晚上干这么晚。

➢ We sell quality food at reasonable prices.
我们卖的食品质量优良, 价格合理。

化 (hua): –*ization* or else

Other than those easy-to-translate 化 expressions, such as *industrialize*, *modernize*, and so on, there are large numbers of 化 expressions that cannot be readily rendered as –*ization* expressions.

More often, a simple adjective can do the trick, or one can use a comparative expression for the same –*ization* effect, as in 干部年轻化, which is actually saying that new leaders should now be younger than the incumbents.

Examples:

➢ 因公用餐要两菜一汤化
For work-related meals, one could only have two dishes and a soup.

➢ 干部要年轻化
Leaders should be younger.

➢ 早餐牛奶化
There should be milk for breakfast.

➢ 领导班子要革命化, 年轻化, 知识化, 专业化。
The leadership should strive to be revolutionary, young, educated, and professional.

➢ 集装箱大型化是以后发展的方向
Larger containers are the future of development.

➢ 卫生宣传要通俗化
The health issues should be made public in plain language.

➢ 现在青少年吸烟已成为社会化问题
Right now, smoking among juveniles has become a social problem.

➢ 这个城市最终走向数字化
This city has finally gone digital.

➢ 在信息化时代, 人的思维方式正在发生巨大的变化。
In the information age, people's way of thinking has undergone profound changes.
(There have been clever renditions for 信息化 now: informationization, informationized; or informatization, informatized.)

活动 (huo dong): *activity* or not

活动 is often used too loosely, added to a verb that has already expressed the activity in question.

In the following cases, one can simply ignore the word 活动 without jeopardizing a faithful rendition.

Examples:

> 医疗服务活动应面向农村。
> Health service should focus on people in the rural area.

> 局长谈如何开展好生产经营管理活动。
> The bureau chief talked about how to put in place effective production and operation management.

> 领导干部要积极参加生产实践活动。
> Leaders must get actively involved in production operations.

> 咨询活动到处可见。
> Consultation service is provided everywhere.

> 连续三周上门服务活动取得了很好的效果。
> The door-to-door service has been going on for three weeks in a row with excellent results.

> 售后服务活动是成功的关键。
> Follow-up service is the key to success.

> 在铁路运输生产实践活动中, 领导要身先士卒。
> Leaders should lead by example in railway transport operations. (The first part of the Chinese sentence is highly repetitive; 生产 实践活动 means the same thing.)

J

机会 (ji hui): *chance* or *opportunity*

The two are often given as the English versions of 机会, but they are not identical twins. There is a difference—a big one.

Simply put, *chance* suggests something accidental, something random, a surprise; something that just happens to be there. Its synonyms include accidental circumstance and unpredictable occasion.

Opportunity suggests something that is expected, planned; something that happens as a result of human efforts. It is more than a chance. Its synonyms include desired circumstance and predictable occasion.

Keep in mind that *opportunity* can include *chance*, but *chance* cannot include *opportunity*.

Let's take a look at how 机会 means something different when translated as *chance* and *opportunity*:

➤ 只是一次偶然的机会, 我遇到了我的前女友。
I met my ex-girlfriend by chance.
(You didn't plan it; it was a surprise. The Chinese words 偶然 help put 机会 in the *chance* camp.)

➤ 这是能遇到你的前女友的好机会
This is a good *opportunity* to meet your ex-girlfriend.
(A circumstance for which you may have planned something else, but it can be used to meet her as well—a plan nonetheless.)

➤ 我今天实在太忙, 没有机会问他。
I was really busy today and didn't have a *chance* to ask him.
(This 机会 is not an occasion you planned; it either came or did not come.)

➤ 我再给你一个机会去问他

I will give you another *opportunity* to ask him.

(This 机会 is treated as an occasion I have arranged for you to ask him.)

➤ 我一直没有机会去问他

I haven't had a *chance* to ask him.

(This 机会 is treated as sheer luck, not part of your plan.)

➤ 只要你努力工作, 就有机会成为组长。

If you work hard, you have the *opportunity* to become a team leader.

(This 机会 is an expected professional growth process.)

➤ 机会总是留给有准备的人的

Opportunities are always reserved for those who are prepared.

(This 机会 is an expected outcome, not an accident.)

➤ 你的机会来了!

Here comes your *opportunity*!

(You have been planning for this moment; the outcome of this 机会 is something you anticipate.)

➤ 你的机会来了!

Here comes your *chance*!

(The moment comes as an accidental occurrence.)

➤ 抓住机会

Seize the *opportunity*.

(This 机会 refers to an anticipated event.)

➤ 抓住机会

Seize the *chance*.

(This 机会 refers to a moment that happens to be available.)

So we translate 就业机会平等 as *equal employment opportunity*, not *equal employment chance*, because 机会 involves government policies, industrial policies, laws, regulations, and rules. It is more than a chance.

Also, *chance meeting* is translated as 偶然相遇 because this *chance* is an accidental event, and the parties happen to run into each other. The Chinese 偶然 captures the unpreparedness beautifully. It is not a meeting previously arranged.

计划 (ji hua): *plan* or *scheme*

First of all, a myth must be debunked. *Scheme* is not a formal version of *plan*. Although the two fall under the same Chinese term 计划, they each express a different sense of 计划.

Scheme is a long-term, systematic 计划; *plan*, relative to *scheme*, is a short-term, step-by-step 计划. Of course, there are five-year plans, a long-term plan, the Marshall Plan, among many other *plans*, nonetheless longer.

Language is never as simple and clear as black and white. Often, personal style gets in the way.

If, in a science document, 计划 is about designing a tool or solving a technical problem, most likely it is *plan*, no matter how grand the topic is.

技术 (ji shu): *technology* or *technique*

These two words may be closely related, but they each express a different concept, albeit they both fall under one Chinese term 技术.

Technology is a study; knowledge of scientific principles of skills and tools. *Technique*, on the other hand, is the specific way of using the technology. So while *technology* is 技术, technique is more 技巧. Different people may use different techniques (技巧) to apply the same technology (技术).

In other words, a smartphone is a technology, but how to use it is a technique. We see technology in airplanes, cameras, and computers, but we see technique in operating them.

Technology in brain surgery involves the latest tools and high-tech equipment. Technique in brain surgery is about doctors' skills in using these tools.

Examples:

➤ 虽然计算机技术发展迅猛, 但是数据输入技术却没有多少变化。
Although computer technology has advanced drastically, the data-entry technique remains almost the same.

➤ 换车轮是个技术活
Changing car tires requires technique (or skill)

➤ 智能手机用的是最先进的通讯技术, 然而, 不是所有的人都掌握充分使用手机的技术。
Smartphones use the most advanced communications technologies, but not all users know the technique of how to make full use of their smartphones.

➤ 他们研究出了一套新的营销技术
They have developed a set of new marketing techniques.

➤ 他成功, 不是因为技术娴熟, 而是因为他执著。
He is successful not because of his superb technique but because of his passion.

➤ 现代医疗技术包括X 光, 核磁共振成像, 等等。
  Modern medical technology includes x-ray and MRI, among others.

➤ 核磁共振成像是技术, 读懂图像也是技术。
  MRI is a technology; understanding the image is a technique.

➤ 当护士三十年, 她练就了一身高超的抽血技术, 病人感觉不到半点疼痛。
  In her thirty years as a nurse, she has developed a superb technique for drawing blood so that patients do not feel any pain.

计算 (ji suan): *calculate* or *compute*

Calculate has its Latin meaning of using small stones, petals, or beans for calculating numbers, as an abacus (算盘) does. So it has to do with arithmetical or mathematical calculation.

Compute, on the other hand, is to calculate in a more complex manner, involving information analyzing, network topology, and protocol, factors that are more than numbers.

Examples:

➤ 经过计算, 系统运转数据与设计数据相符。
  Computation shows that the operation data matches the design data.
  (Assuming 计算 involves more than working out numbers)
Or
  Calculation shows that the operation data matches the design data.
  (Assuming 计算 involves mathematical operation.)

➤ 您可以计算出您最佳退休年月

Through calculation, you can find the best year to retire.

(This assumes 计算 involves mathematical operation, including interest rates, inflation rates, years remaining on the job, and the like.)

Or

Through computation, you can find the best year to retire.

(This assumes 计算 involves retirement policies, health conditions, economic health, demographic changes, and marital status, among other factors.)

➤ 为了计算一颗卫星的准确位置, 所有关键数据必须齐全。

One needs all the critical data to compute the exact position of a satellite.

(Here, 计算 must involve coordinates, parameters, and other values, as well as numbers.)

坚持 (jian chi): *insist* or *persist* or *something else*

There are three different 坚持.

First坚持: *insist,* as in 我们不同意他一个人去, 可他坚持要去 (We didn't want him to go there alone, but he insisted on going all by himself.) This坚持is saying, "I want to do it my way, no matter what." Its Chinese cousins include 执意, 非要 … 不可.

Second坚持: *adhere to, follow,* as in 坚持自己的看法 (*stick to one's opinion*); 坚持党的路线 (*follow the Party's line*); 坚持改革开放 (*adhere to the opening-up and reform policy*). The second坚持 doesn't have the stubbornness of the first one.

Third坚持: *persist,* as in 他一直坚持寻找, 最后终于找到答案了 (He persisted in the search and finally found the answer). This

坚持 expresses determination, perseverance. Its cousins include 坚持不懈, 一如既往, 坚忍不拔.

Examples:

➤ 我们都说不可能, 可他坚持认为可能。
We all said it was impossible, but he insisted it was possible.

➤ 我真地不想去, 可他坚持要去。
I really didn't want to go, but he insisted we go.

➤ 他坚持认为他一点也不知情。
He insisted on his innocence.

➤ 她妈妈坚持让我跟她女儿一起走。
Her mother insisted that I go with her daughter.

➤ 尽管天气炎热, 队员们还是坚持训练。
The players continued with their training, in spite of the scorching heat.

➤ 我们要坚持改革方针, 继续开放金融市场。
We must adhere to the reform policy and continue to open up financial markets to the world.
(To say "*insist on* the reform policy" indicates that *people are against it, but you want to do it regardless.* It is more like saying, 我们非要坚持改革方针不可. This is not the intended message.)

➤ 我们要坚持科学发展的道路
We must keep to the path of scientific development.

(Similarly, "insist on the path" would mean 我们执意, 非要走科学发展的道路不可.)

> 我们要坚持和完善人民代表大会制度
> We must uphold and improve the system of People's Congress.
> (Similarly, "insist on upholding and improving the system of People's Congress" would mean, 我们执意, 非要完善人民代表大会制度不可.)

> 我坚持一年看三本小说
> I made an effort to read three novels a year.
> (I never gave up the effort.)

Or

I insisted on reading three novels a year.
(No one believed I could do it, but I stood my ground. Translated back into Chinese, it says, 我非要一年看三本小书不可.)

> 他坚持认为他是无辜的
> He insists that he is innocent.

Or

He insisted on his innocence.
(Other people don't believe he is innocent, but he believes himself, regardless.)

> 只要坚持, 就能成功。
> Persist in your efforts, and you will succeed.

Or

Don't give up, and you will succeed.

健康 (jian kang): *healthy* or *healthful*

健康 is a translation issue only when it is used in the context of improving health, as in 你们吃得很健康; 健康小吃, and the like.

So is it "You should eat healthy food," or "You should eat healthful food"? Or is it *healthy snack* or *healthful snack*?

I am sure you hear *healthy food* a lot more than *healthful food*. After all, the former sounds natural.

But if the ongoing battle over the usage of *healthy* and *healthful* is any indication, it clearly shows that people believe the pair exists for a reason, and they each have a distinct meaning: while *healthy* means "free of disease," *healthful* means "beneficial to health."

In other words, *healthy* is about a good condition, as in *a healthy plant, a healthy child*. *Healthful* is about being conducive to good health, as in a *healthful diet*.

Healthy is 状况良好, 没有毛病; *healthful* is 有利健康, 对身体好. Clearly, *good condition* and *improving condition* are two different things.

A jar of snow-white, odorless lard tells you the pork fat is *healthy* (in sound condition, ready to cook), but it may not be *healthful* (may raise blood cholesterol levels) to one who, per doctor's warning, should cut down on saturated fat.

So to answer the question 健康小吃 above, is it *healthy snack* or *healthful snack*? Answer: *healthful snack*, although it may sound a bit, say, professorial.

Should you care how it sounds? Maybe you should, if you don't want your translation to offend usage-sensitive readers.

The 健康 translations below help set the pair apart:

➤ 你应该换一个健康的生活方式
You should change to a healthy/healthful lifestyle.
(Here, *healthy* and *healthful* are found used interchangeably. Reason: if the lifestyle is *healthy*—be positive, smile a lot, meet

new friends, help people, exercise, keep a healthful diet—then it is good for your health; thus, it is *healthful*.)

➤ 大夫督促年轻的家长们, 要让刚会走路的孩子们吃健康的早饭, 而不是图容易, 给孩子们吃罐头食品。
Doctors urge young parents to feed their toddlers healthful breakfasts instead of quick-to-fix canned food.

Luckily, when 健康 is *not* used in the context of being beneficial to health, the translation is clear: *healthy*. As in,

➤ 健康的心态
Healthy state of mind

➤ 健康的运作机制
Healthy operation mechanism

➤ 健康的树苗
Healthy tree saplings

建设 (jian she): *construction* or something else

建设 is used in more places than you can imagine, but not every 建设 is *construction*. In the English language, *construction* (or its verb, *construct*) often means industrial or engineering projects, such as building roads, bridges, and so forth.

So when 军队建设 is rendered as *military construction*, readers might assume you are talking about *building military facilities*. When 国防建设 is translated as *defense construction,* it means *building defense facilities*, such as missile defense systems, air defense systems, and counter-terrorism systems.

In English, the word *construction* often suggests economic activities, be it developing mines, building infrastructures, hydropower dams, building highways, engineering projects, and the like.

So when 经济建设 is translated to *economic construction*, English speakers would hear "some building projects in the economy." It is saying something, but what is it trying to say?

At any rate, there is a good reason to translate 经济建设 as *economic construction*, or vice versa.

In 1931, the Conference of Business Executives was held in Moscow. Joseph Stalin delivered his keynote speech to the conference, "New Conditions—New Tasks in Economic Construction,"[3] thus giving *economic construction* a unique meaning in the socialist camp--what the West would say was *building the economy*.

This may be the reason why 经济建设 is readily translated to *economic construction* among Chinese linguists.

Economic construction for 经济建设 may sound all right for certain group of readers; but for others, *building the economy* gets the message across beautifully.

Examples:

➢ 中国这几十年一直致力于经济建设

For the past decades, China has committed itself to economic development.

➢ 我们要加强国防建设

We must strengthen national defense.

(*Defense construction* could easily be mistaken as defense facilities, such as missile launch sites and so forth.)

---

[3] https://www.marxists.org/reference/archive/stalin/works/1931/06/23.htm; accessed December 12, 2014

➤ 领导班子要重视员工的政治思想建设
The leadership should make a sincere effort in equipping staff with correct political ideas.

➤ 我们要加强领导班子的建设
We must double our efforts in building an effective leadership.

➤ 铁路建设是今后五年的工作重点
Developing the railway industry will be the focus of our work for the next five years.
(*Railway construction* would mean building rail tracks, rail cars, and train stations.)

➤ 市场建设是关乎经济发展的大事
Building market mechanisms is of important significance to economic development.
(*Market construction* could mean zoning off a piece of land, building booths and loading docks, and so forth.)

➤ 各级领导要重视党的建设。
Leaders at all levels must give importance to strengthening the leadership of the Party.

➤ 这些管理标准突出了机关的政治建设
These management standards highlight the political agenda of the agency.

结合 (jie he): *combine* or something else

结合 has two meanings. It can mean *join two or more things*, as in 我和她结合在一起; 将几种材料结合在一起. In these cases, one can use *combine*, *link*, and *integrate*.

It also means *take something into consideration*. In this case, *combine* is a poor translation for 结合.

Examples:

> 如果我们将两组人马结合起来, 我们就有了一支最有竞争力的团队。
>
> If we combine the two teams, we will have a most competitive team.

> 管理人员应结合市场情况, 研究公司的运作策略。
>
> Managers should incorporate market situations in their studies of the company's operation strategies.

Or

Managers should take into account market situations when examining the company's operation strategies.

> 我们要结合他的工作表现, 考虑是否给他加薪
>
> We should take a look at his performance when deciding whether to give him a raise.

> 实际操作也可结合具体训练课题进行
>
> Hands-on operation can be done by integrating it with specific training subjects.

> ➢ 员工的营销训练要与产品性能, 市场需求紧密结合。
> Staff's marketing training should revolve around products' features and market demands.

> ➢ 本文结合早期的科研结果, 深刻分析了信息市场的变化。
> With early research findings taken into consideration, this article offers a profound analysis of the changes in the information market.

解决 (jie jue): *solve, resolve* or something else

Often, dictionaries would give you *solve* or *resolve* for 解决. In some cases, however, you should give it a second thought before choosing *solve* or *resolve*.

First of all, *solve* and *resolve* are not identical twins. There is a subtle difference.

Generally, *solve* is collated with *problems* and *resolve* with *issues*. *Solve* is more often used in addressing math problems, puzzles, and the like that involve a clear, straightforward answer.

Resolve is more often used in addressing issues that frequently involve negotiation, discussion, compromise, agreement or disagreement, or understanding or misunderstanding.

So *solve* is often found in math, technical, or accounting matters. *Resolve* is often used in social, international, or political matters or conflicts, assuming clear-cut solutions are hard to come by in these issues.

Therefore, 解决数学问题 renders as *solve a math problem*, but 解决社会问题 would better be *resolve social issues*.

For 解决 in other expressions, we need to work around *solve* or *resolve*.

Examples:

➢ 我们终于成功地解决了精确定位, 可靠导航等关键技术。
We have finally made successful breakthroughs in the critical technologies such as precision positioning and reliable navigation.

Or

We have finally successfully acquired the critical technologies such as precision positioning and reliable navigation.
(We don't *solve* technologies—we acquire/apply them, but we solve technological problems.)

➢ 社会工作者要解决好主动询问和被动解答的关系
Social workers must properly handle the relationship between actively inquiring and reactively answering questions.
(We don't *solve* relationships; we handle/manage them.)

➢ 我们首先要解决的任务是基础训练
The first task we must take on is basic training.
(We don't *solve* tasks; we finish/complete them.)

➢ 这个软件可以解决各类系统分析
This software can handle various system analyses.
(We don't *solve* analysis; we conduct/perform/make analysis.)

➢ 为了盖多功能教学楼, 首先要解决楼的设计原理。
To build a multifunction building, the school must first address its design principles. (We don't *solve* principles; we follow/establish them.)

➢ 建造此类系统所需的能力尚待解决
The capabilities for building this type of system have yet to be acquired.
(We don't *solve* capabilities; we acquire them.)

介绍 (jie shao): *introduction to* or *introduction of*

The problem is not in *introduction* but in the use of *to* and *of*, a challenge to non-native English speakers.

One is less likely to go wrong when translating 介绍 as a verb, as in 介绍在座的来宾 (introduce the guests present today), 介绍一本畅销书 (introduce a best-seller), but it is when translating its noun form *introduction* that mistakes occur.

Mistakes often happen when one uses *introduction of* where *introduction to* should be used.

Simply put, *introduction to* is 介绍; *introduction of* is 引进

Examples:

➤ 这项新技术的引进大大提高了效率
Introduction of the new technology greatly improved efficiency.
(*Introduction to the new technology* means 这个提案的介绍.)

➤ 没有人关心我开始对这个提案的介绍
No one was interested in my introduction to the proposal in the beginning.
(*Introduction of the proposal* means 这个提案的引进.)

Note: The only place where *introduction* is used to mean 介绍, unmistakably, is in the following two usages:

➤ 这本书的介绍部分写得简明易懂
The introduction part of the book is simple and clear.
Or
The introduction of the book is simple and clear

Please note in the first example, *part* is part of *of*, thereby freeing it from being mistaken as 引进; in the second example, *introduction* is blessed by the clear context, namely it is a section of the book, again freeing it from being mistaken as 引进, in spite of its "introduction of" structure.

进入/ 进到 (jin ru or jin dao): *enter* or *enter into*

Case 1: *enter into the room* (wrong)
Case 2: *enter the room* (correct)
Case 3: *enter the twenty-first century* (correct)
Case 4: *enter into an agreement* (correct)

Case 1: The problem is more common among native Chinese speakers. Somehow, the use of *come into*, *go into*, *slip into*, *walk into*, *run into* a physical location leads to the next logical use of *enter into*. There is logic behind 进 and入: *enter* for 进, and *into* for 入.

But this is a poor logic. The rule for *enter*, in the sense of 进入, is *never* use *into*.

Case 2: 进入/进到 physical locations, simply say,

➢ enter the building
➢ enter the office
➢ enter the yard
➢ enter the house

For this rule, however, there is an exception. In translation, when 进入 must be rendered as *entry,* the noun form of *enter*, as dictated by the English structure, *into* must be used, even if 进入 pertains to entering a physical location. Therefore:

69

> 外婆是怎么进到我的卧室的?
>
> How did Grandma get her entry into my bedroom?

> 他是怎么进入美国的, 至今仍是个谜。
>
> His entry into the US still remains a mystery.

> 他们最后还是获准进入法庭。
>
> They were finally granted entry into the courtroom.

> 他们不准进入古巴
>
> They were denied entry into Cuba.

Case 3: For 进入/进到 nonphysical, figurative locations, such as time period, market, life, and the like, use *enter* without *into*.

> 我们进入了一个新的时代
>
> We are now entering a new era.

Or

We are now embarking on a new era.

> 我们进入了一个全新的领域
>
> We are now entering uncharted waters.

Or

We are now stepping into in a brand-new field.

> 我们进入了一个繁荣昌盛时期
>
> We entered a period of prosperity.

Or

We are now embarking on a period of prosperity.

> 千万不要进入已经饱和了的市场
>
> Never enter a saturated market.

> ➢ 她走进了我的生活/世界/心房
> She entered my life/world/heart.

> ➢ 这些熊已经进入了冬眠期
> These bears are now entering a hibernation stage.

Or

These bears are now going into hibernation.

There must be a place for *enter into*, after all. Yes, there is, in case 4. It simply means *signing an agreement, treaty,* or *contract* or *starting a relationship.*

In translation, where *enter into* is rendered, the Chinese terms are 签署, 签订; therefore, mistranslating 进入/进来 is not the issue. Below are a few *enter into* examples, just for the fun of it:

> ➢ Enter into an agreement 签署协议
> ➢ Enter into a contract 签订合同
> ➢ Enter into a strategic relationship 建立战略关系
> ➢ Enter into a long-term partnership 开始一个长期伙伴关系

进行 (jin xing): *carry out, perform, conduct,* or none of them

In most cases, 进行is part of the 对 … 进行structure, where 进行 is a structural element so a Chinese sentence will flow nicely.

In many other cases, 进行 has been used too freely, rendering it unnecessary to translate. In most cases, 进行 is counterproductive in semantics.

Therefore, one can simply ignore 进行 and still get the message across beautifully.

Let's take a look at how 进行 is used—or rather, abused:

➤ 某歌手在淡出歌坛几年后, 曾努力**进行**复出, 但并不成功。
➤ 组委邀请了著名演员到现场**进行**评判。
➤ 调试后, 再**进行**按钮。
➤ 由于篇幅有限, 笔者就不再**进行**一一论述。
➤ 对选手**进行**支持的人请亮牌。
➤ 中国馆也有高科技展品**进行**展出。
➤ 要在腹部顺时针**进行**轻揉。
➤ 观众有机会见到主持人选择不同的一方**进行**主持。

Now, you get the picture.

Take out 进行, and you can still read on with no problem.

I cannot think of any meaningful reason why people must use 进行 in these expressions.

It has butchered the language for sure.

经济 (jing ji): *economy* or something else

This is one of the classic cases where you will find dictionaries are not much help.

Dictionaries often use *economy* for 经济 to express 国民经济, 经济活动, 经济利益, 经济增长, 经济环境 and the like. In these cases, 经济 expresses economic activities on a national level.

Against this big economic picture, it is all right to translate 经济 as economic/economy, as in:

✓ 不论其经济条件如何, 都有上学的权利
   No one should be denied education, regardless of his or her economic situation.
✓ 学校应该接受来自不同经济背景的学生

Educational institutions should welcome students from all economic walks of life.

In other cases, 经济 may suggest financial situations. One needs other words to translate 经济 in order for the expression to flow well.

Examples:

➢ 他家的经济条件比较好。
He is from a well-to-do family.

➢ 今年我厂的经济状况很好。
Our factory is financially sound this year.

➢ 自从我丈夫失业后，我们的经济负担比从前重了很多。
Ever since my husband lost his job, our financial burden has become heavier.

➢ 他很有经济头脑。
He has great business sense.

Please note, 经济 also means *less expensive, cheap*; its adjective form is *economical*, not *economic*.

Some online dictionaries incorrectly translate 经济考虑 as *economical consideration*. But, what 经济考虑 is trying to indicate are considerations or policies that have to do with the economy, not *cheap considerations*.

Mistakes like this are often due to carelessness.

➢ 这个办法既经济又实惠
This approach is both economical and practical.

> 这个工具具有灵活, 经济, 耐用的特点。
> This tool offers the advantages of versatility, economy, and durability.

经济效益 (jing ji xiao yi): *economic benefit, profit,* or *economic efficiency*

经济效益 is often translated as *economic benefit,* but a close look at the context in which 经济效益 is used, and one would find it does not always mean *economic benefit.*

In its various contexts, 经济效益 should have three renditions:

Rendition1: *economic benefit*—something is done to benefit the economy as a whole. Its expanded Chinese expression would be 国民经济从中获益.

Rendition 2: *make a profit* (获得利润, 赚钱).

Rendition 3: *economic efficiency* (经济效率), meaning making profits in the most cost-effective way.

Let's take a look at how 经济效益as *economic benefit* (rendition 1) is used in English contexts:

> Ten years of record immigration to Britain has produced virtually no *economic benefits* for the country.
> (Immigrants' contribution to the economy was canceled out by their use of society's resources, such as education and health care, among others.)

> The Disability Act can have huge *economic benefits* for society.
> (Under this law, people with disabilities can find employment, become independent, and support themselves and their families; thus, the nation's economy will benefit from their increased purchasing power.)

➢ An *economic benefit* assessment is done on California's investment in the transportation infrastructure.
(This indicates how much California's economy will benefit from the investment in transportation infrastructure.)

➢ The publications highlight the *economic benefits* of pre-kindergarten programs in terms of future achievement, social engagement, and productivity.
(Good pre-kindergarten programs can successfully prepare small children for their future success, which will benefit the nation's economy in future.)

➢ The studies clearly demonstrate the *economic benefits* of improved long-range weather forecasting.
(This weather forecasting can pre-warn businesses against unfavorable weather conditions, thus avoiding damages and losses.)

The above samples suggest that the nation's economy benefits from the efforts in question.

By extension, there are also *political benefits, financial benefits, technical benefits, academic benefits, educational benefits, military benefits, humanitarian benefits, psychological benefits, commercial benefits, trade benefits,* and the like, all suggesting benefits to these areas as a result of something being done.

The following Chinese expressions can also give an excellent illustration for 经济效益:

➢ 新建的电动汽车厂将会给本州带来100 亿美元的经济效益
The new electric car factory will produce $10 billion in economic impact to the state.

➤ 公司对这个项目的每 $1 投资, 都会产生 $50的经济效益
For every $1 the company invests, the project will generate $50 in economic impact.

Next, let's take a look at how 经济效益, as *make a profit* (rendition 2), is used:

➤ 我们厂的目标是产生最大的经济效益和社会效益。
Our factory's objective is to create maximum *profits* and contributions to the well-being of society.

➤ 我公司今年的经济效益很好。
Our company has made a good *profit* this year.

➤ 员工的工资要和企业的经济效益挂钩。
Employees' salaries should be linked with the company's *profits*.

➤ 工厂今年的经济效益不太好, 所以奖金不多。
The factory has not made much *profit* this year, so our bonus is very small.

➤ 该产品效率高, 质量好, 具有可观的经济效益。
This product demonstrates high efficiency and excellent quality and is tremendously *profitable*.

➤ 让年轻人上春晚, 这纯粹是为了收视率, 为了经济效益。
Letting young artists appear at the annual Spring Festival Gala is purely out of the concern for increasing viewing rate and *profit*.

Simply put, if 经济效益 is about making a profit, then it should be translated as such. Gone are the days when making money was considered bourgeois; therefore, bad.

Let's take a look at how 经济效益, as *economic efficiency* (rendition 3), is used:

➤ 董事会要求我们两年内以最小的投入争取最大的经济效益。
The board of directors requires that we increase *economic efficiency* with the lowest possible investment in two years.

➤ 裁员后, 经济效益有大幅度的提升。
Following downsizing, *economic efficiency* has increased a great deal.

➤ 公司的经济效益如何与管理是否科学有很大关系。
The company's *economic efficiency* has a lot to do with whether it is managed in a scientific way.

➤ 提高经济效益, 意味着提高投资效益和资源利用效益。
Increasing *economic efficiency* means increasing both investment efficiency and resource-use efficiency.

To express similar meanings, there are *administrative efficiency, management efficiency, energy efficiency, residential efficiency, organizational efficiency*, and so forth.

Simply put, if 经济效益 is about a cost-effective way to achieve an objective, then it should be *economic efficiency*.

精确 / 精准 (jing que / jing zhun): *precision* or *accuracy*

It is not that *precision* is more accurate or precise than *accuracy*. Rather, they each express a different concept of 精确 (精准).

Let's look at two categories: the science of measurement and non-science situations.

In the science of measurement, they each measure against a different value. *Precision* is about multiple measurements (or results) being close to each other (if not an exact match).

In a soccer game, for example, one kicks the ball ten times to the goal, each time sending it about an inch over the crossbar. We say the player kicks with *precision* but not *accuracy*. In all ten kicks, the player swings his leg at the same angle, with the same force, at the same distance to the goal, sending the ball at the same angle to the crossbar.

In this case, the "measurement" is that range of "about an inch above the crossbar." By "measurements (or results) close to each other," it is meant that all ten kicks sent the ball flying over the crossbar at about the same range: the first kick, 0.9 inch; the second, 0.8 inch; the third, 1 inch; the fourth, 1.02 inch; the fifth, 0.85 inch, and so forth.

Accuracy, on the other hand, is about measurement against a given value: kicking the ball into the goal. For a kick with *accuracy*, one must send the ball into the goal. He made ten kicks, each with different force and from a different angle, but all ten kicks sent the ball into the goal—some flying right into the goal, some bouncing back in from the bar, some slipping through the goalie's hands but in nonetheless.

Simply put, *precision* is more about *how* an action is executed—how the ball is kicked each time. *Accuracy* is more about the *result* of the action—kicking the ball into the goal.

Of course, *precision* and *accuracy* often are the two sides of a coin. How an action is executed determines the desired result, but for the sake of argument, let's put the two in extreme cases for the time being.

In a non-science situation, let's take machine translation, for example. The computer is programmed to translate 对 as *to be correct*, and the computer does so faithfully every time it comes across 对.

Such translation of 对 is *precise*, until one day it comes across 一对恋人 (two lovers). The computer continues to translate对 faithfully, as it has done hundreds of times before, and translates "One is correct lover" for 一对恋人.

The result: not accurate.

So, *precision* refers to performing a programmed function, time and time and time again, and producing the same result. In this case, 对 is rendered as *correct* each and every time. In the case of soccer game above, the ball flies over the crossbar each and every time.

Accuracy, on the other hand, is about the result matching a given value, namely 一对. In this case, 对 is a part of the phrase 一对. An accurate translation must match the given value: *two* or *a pair*.

So if 精确 (精准) is about how a programmed function is performed, then 精确 (精准) can be safely rendered as *precision* (*precise*)—translating 对 to *correct* each time, regardless of whether it is part of 一对.

But if 精确 (精准) is about a result—namely, matching a given value—then 精确 (精准) can be safely translated to *accuracy* (*accurate*). It is accurate to translate对 as *correct* each time when 对 expresses an affirmation and to translate 对 as *pair/two* when 对 is a part of 一对.

Here are two examples to highlight the difference:

➢ *The doctor closes the bleeding vessel with precision.*

It is saying that the doctor is doing it as he/she is trained to do, following every single step by the book, as he/she has done hundreds of times before.

➢ *The doctor closes the bleeding vessel with accuracy.*

It is saying that the doctor finds the bleeding vessel in no time, among a maze of blood-stained vessels and tissues.

Of course, for all practical purposes, *precision* and *accuracy* are often intended to serve each other. So to make sure the bleeding is stopped, not only should the doctor find the vessel (*accuracy*), but he/she must also do it correctly (*precision*).

Again, in the case of machine translation, to ensure the computer translates对correctly (*accuracy*), it is so programmed that it checks whether 对 is an affirmation or part of 一对, and it does so each and every time, faithfully (*precision*).

Examples:

➢ 精确打击武器
Precision strike weapons
(It is about the programmed functions that dictate what the weapons will hit.)

➢ 精确的天气预报
Accurate weather forecast
(It is about the result—rain or shine—not how the forecast is done.)

➢ 提高测量水深的精度
Improve water-depth measurement accuracy and precision
(It is about two things: how [precision] water depth is measured and the actual water depth [result].)

➢ 新船下水前, 要确保水深的精确度。
Ensure water-depth accuracy before the new ship launches.
(It is about a fact—water depth.)

➢ 精确 (准确) 的英文翻译
Accurate translation

(It is about the result. An English version is given as a reference. The translation is measured against the English version.)

> 飞机必须精确地降落在甲板上两条白线以内
> Aircraft must land precisely within the two white lines on the deck.

Or

Aircraft must land with precision within the two white lines on the deck.

(It is about how the aircraft lands. The pilot is trained to land the bird somewhere near the middle section of the marked runway.)

K

宽带 (kuan dai): *broadband* or *wideband*

It has to do with what *broadband* and *wideband* are all about. Simply put, speed is what separates the two.

Wideband is a much faster connection. It is the next generation of Internet high-speed connection.

So the context in which 宽带 is used dictates whether it is *broadband* or *wideband*.

L

理解/ 懂 (li jie/dong): *understand* or *comprehend*

Does *comprehend* indicate a deeper understanding than *understand*? Absolutely not. The difference, if any, is less about meaning and more about style.

The history of the English language tells an interesting story. The English people had been using *understand* until 1066, when the Normans invaded England and brought with them *comprehend*, a French version of *understand*.

Since the Normans dominated England's high society, *comprehend* was thus used more in courts, governments, churches, educational institutions, and the like.

We now have *comprehend* for formal occasions and *understand* for everyday conversation. It is all a matter of style, much like the distinction between 理解 and 懂.

The key to proper translation of 理解 is correct identification of the style (or tone) in 理解. If 理解 is used in a formal occasion or on a serious subject, then *comprehend* is a perfect choice; otherwise, use *understand*.

Examples:

➤ 我无法理解人体复杂的神经系统

I find it impossible to comprehend the complicated human nerve systems.

(It may be a statement by, say, a professor.)

Or

I find it impossible to understand the complicated human nerve systems.

(It may be a statement by, say, a college student.)

➤ 请你理解我的一片好心

Please try to understand my good intentions.

(It has a conversational tone.)

灵活 (ling huo): *flexible, versatile, nimble, agile,* and many more

The above choices are just a few among many. Check translation examples, and you will find different 灵活 renditions, such as 他脑筋灵活 (He is quick) and 车轮灵活 (Wheels turn easily), not to mention *flexible,* as in 时间灵活 (flexible schedule) and 政策灵活 (flexible policy), the most frequently used version of 灵活.

But *flexible* cannot cover all 灵活.

Flexible for 灵活: in non-technical contexts, we see that 灵活 means "easy to adapt to changes," often translated in contexts such as *flexible schedule, flexible approach, flexible foreign policy, flexible program,* and the like.

In science, however, *flexible* often has a specific meaning: capable of bending, as in *flexible tree branches, flexible leather material, flexible ruler, flexible antenna, flexible clothes hanger.*

➤ 手术后, 她的手指灵活多了!

Her fingers are much more flexible as a result of the operation! (Meaning: fingers can bend after surgery.)

Nimble for灵活: in the same "手术后" context above, the same sentence can take on an interesting twist if translated otherwise.

➤ 手术后, 她的手指灵活多了!

Her fingers are much more nimble as a result of the operation. (*Nimble fingers,* in this case, says more than the ability to bend; it is about the ability to perform delicate functions, such as sign language signs.)

➤ 她织毛衣时, 手指真灵活!
Her fingers are so nimble when knitting sweaters!
(Meaning: fingers can move swiftly between loops, yarn, and needles. One may also see 手指真灵巧 instead of 灵活. In this case, there would not be the problem of mistranslation灵活 as *flexible.*)

Versatile for 灵活: it often denotes resourcefulness, the ability to perform multiple tasks.

➤ 他虽然生下来就没有双臂, 可是他的脚趾非常灵活。
Although he was born without two arms, his toes are extremely versatile.
(*Versatile* expresses more than simply bending and quick movement; it implies the ability to perform multiple functions, including writing with a pen, typing on a computer keyboard, brushing teeth, and even changing car tires.)

Agile for 灵活: it also denotes quick and easy movement. Its closest cousin is 灵敏, 敏捷.

➤ 那只小猴子真灵活!
That baby monkey is very agile!
(It runs and jumps with much ease.)

Translating it as "That baby monkey is very flexible!" runs the risk of misleading readers to read that the baby monkey adapts to the environment easily, surviving equally well both in a cage and in the mountains.

Of course, if 灵敏 or 敏捷, instead of 灵活, appears in the above expression, one would not have the headache of finding the proper word for 灵活.

Below are various translations for 灵活 without using the suggested choices above:

➤ 这个把手转动很灵活
The handle turns freely.

➤ 他机智灵活
He is very sharp.

➤ 他灵活机动
He is tactful.

➤ 这个车在山路上开很灵活
The car is easy to drive on mountain roads.

➤ 他的做法很灵活
His approach is highly adaptable.

M

矛盾 (mao dun): *contradiction, problem* or something else

矛盾 is often readily translated into *contradiction*. It is correct only when used to express something illogical or inconsistent—things that are mutually exclusive.

The correct use of *contradiction* is best illustrated in the following sentence: *You said you have a loving heart, but you chose to ignore the poor old lady who asked for help!*

Such is a *contradiction*.

The most common error in translating 矛盾 as *contradiction* is in this phrase: 供需矛盾 *contradiction between supply and demand*. Supply and demand are not mutually exclusive; on the contrary, they need each other. *Demand* creates a market for *supply*; *supply* feeds *demand*. There is no contradiction. They coexist. This 矛盾 is not *contradiction*; it is *imbalance*.

Simply put, when it is not about a mutually exclusive matter, 矛盾 is simply 问题, or a problem.

Examples (where 矛盾 is *contradiction*):

➢ 你们的观点相互矛盾
Your arguments contradict each other.

➢ 你的解释充满了矛盾
Your explanations are full of contradictions.

➢ 关于这件事, 我们听到了前后矛盾的说法
We have heard contradictory accounts of the incident.

> 他们得出的两个结论完全矛盾
>
> They had reached two completely contradictory conclusions.

Examples (where 矛盾 is not *contradiction*):

> 可以看出, 他此刻心里是矛盾的
>
> Apparently, he is struggling at the moment.

> 目前最好的解决办法是将矛盾上交
>
> The best solution now is to pass the problem to the management.

> 要研究经济领域矛盾运动的一般规律
>
> One must study the general law of interaction between various problems in the economic sector.

> 要妥善处理他们之间的矛盾
>
> One must properly handle the conflicts (disagreements, grudges, problems) between the two of them.

> 双方的矛盾很深, 很难一时沟通。
>
> The two sides hold deep grudges against each other; it will be hard for them to bridge their differences any time soon.

> 现在市场上, 供需矛盾突出, 人民情绪不稳。
>
> The market is now seeing serious imbalance between supply and demand, and people are becoming restless.

目标 (mu biao): *goal or objective*

They are both listed under 目标. Not much help for translation. *Goal* or *objective*—what's the difference?

Basically, *goals* are about bigger, general plans; *objectives* are about small, specific steps toward the goals. *Goals* are long term; *objectives* are short term.

In a company's business meeting, one often hears the CEO urge his deputies to set goals. He or she warns them that a goal without objectives can never be achieved, and objectives without a goal won't get the company where it wants to be.

We see *objectives* in résumés. They are specific, concrete steps to achieve something.

We see *goals* in long-term, lifetime plans. They are general, grand, hard-to-pinpoint plans.

Knowing these differences can help us translate 目标 accurately, assuming the Chinese 目标 also expresses a similar difference.

Examples:

➢ 我们要以坚定的步伐迈向预定的目标
We must soldier on toward the designated goals.
(It is not about specific steps. The 目标 is general.)

➢ 这是我的目标: 两年内拿到学位, 然后找个工作.
This is my objective: finish my degree in two years and then find a job.

模仿 (mo fang): *imitate* or *emulate*

Granted, we have *simulate* for 仿真. It won't pose a problem. But 模仿 is a different story.

Basically, both *imitate* and *emulate* are saying the same thing: reproduce an act. They are both found under the entry of 模仿 with no distinction, but there is an important difference.

Imitate simply means reproduction of, say, an act, as in, my little brother imitates a dog bark; my pet parrot imitates my iPhone's ringtone; he imitates the way I talk.

But *emulate* expresses an ambition, an aspiration, a goal. One not only *imitates* an act of a person but aspires to be as successful as the person. Its Chinese synonym is 效仿 or 仿效. *Imitate* doesn't have that tone of aspiration.

So the following translations of 模仿 would render different meanings:

> 他要模仿他当空军的哥哥样子, 以后去开战斗机。
> He wants to *emulate* his air force brother and fly a fighter jet one day.
> (The emphasis is not on imitating any acts but on following in his brother's footsteps to become a fighter jet pilot.)

A word-savvy reader may use 效仿 instead of 模仿. This would alert the translator to use *emulate*. Problem solved!

Not all Chinese expressions are word savvy, nor is every word chosen carefully. A translator still faces the hard battle of correct word choice.

> 他常常模仿他当空军的哥哥, 想长大后也开飞机。
> He often *imitates* his air force brother, hoping to fly an aircraft when he grows up.
> (He sits in an imaginary cockpit, touching imaginary instruments, and making the roaring sound of an aircraft taking off.)

Put simply, if you are writing play after play, you are *emulating* great playwrights like Shakespeare, but if you have long hair, you are *imitating* Shakespeare.

If you are training hard on a basketball court, you are *emulating* Yao Ming or Michael Jordan, but if you talk in a low voice, you are *imitating* them.

P

评估 (ping gu): *assessment* or *evaluation* or *appraisal*

Look up 评估 in dictionaries, and you will find *assessment, evaluation,* and *appraisal* (or their verb forms, *assess, evaluate, appraise*), all thrown to you. But the three are not interchangeable. They are different.

Simply put, *assessment* addresses *what*, and *evaluation* addresses *how*. *Assessment* is more like its Chinese cousins 估算, 估计, 审察, whereas *evaluation* is more like 评价, 评判, 评审.

But *appraisal* is a bit different. In American English, it is mostly about financial, monetary issues, meaning to set a price on something, much like 估价. In British English, it is used the same way as *evaluation* or *assessment*.

Examples:

➢ 在他的假释期间, 他必须定期作酗酒评估。
During his probation, he has to go through a periodic alcohol-abuse assessment.
(It is about *how much alcohol* he has used in a given period of time: a bottle, half a bottle, a cup, etc.)
Or
During his probation, he has to go through an alcohol-abuse evaluation.

(It is about checking the *effectiveness* of his alcohol abuse: how many times he has passed out.)

> 通过回答一些问题，能对机器可能过热的问题得到比较准确的评估。

  By answering a list of questions, one can get a fairly accurate assessment of potential machine-overheating problems.

  (It is about *what the problems are*, with a list of problems presented.)

Or

  By answering a list of questions, one can get a fairly accurate evaluation of potential machine-overheating problems.

  (It is about *how seriously the problems have affected the machine*, as if the problems were designed to cause problems, and now is the time to check the designed result.)

> 当地政府派出一批专家，对地震造成的损害做出评估。

  The local government sent out a group of experts to assess the earthquake damage.

  ("Damage assessment" says *what the damages are*—collapsed buildings, broken pipelines, fallen power lines, and so forth.)

Or

  The local government sent out a group of experts to evaluate the earthquake damages.

  ("Damage evaluation" would suggest that a host of damage factors are designed to cause damages, and now the government is checking *whether they have done what they were designed for*. Or, to stretch the imagination a bit further, the earth was programmed to rock at a given time. Now we need to see how effectively the earth rocked itself as designed to cause the damages.)

> 部门经理对本部门员工的工作评估很满意。

The department head is quite satisfied with the staff's performance evaluation.

(How the staff is doing)

Or

The department head is quite satisfied with the staff's performance assessment.

(What the staff is supposed to do)

> 就业局势评估

Employment situation assessment

(What the situation looks like—how many people have been employed; how many potential job openings will be available; what jobs are available, and the like)

Or

Employment situation evaluation

(How employment works—how a given employment policy has been working.)

Q

启示 (qi shi): *enlightenment, implication* or something else

Enlightenment is often found as the ready choice for 启示. In most cases, 启示 is simply saying *what something means*, or *what something tells us*. Its Chinese synonym is 意味着什么, whereas *enlightenment* is too big a word and is better reserved for 启发, 教诲, 启迪, 启蒙.

Enlightenment in the following cases would sound awkward, to say the least.

➢ 此次卢布贬值对中国市场有什么启示
What the current ruble devaluation means to the Chinese market

➢ APEC 蓝给我们什么启示?
What does the APEC Blue tell us?

➢ 老师, 这个题怎么答, 能给我个启示吗?
Teacher, can you give me some hints on how to solve this problem?
Or
Teacher, can you give me some ideas on how to approach this problem?

➢ 这个案子给我们的启示是什么?
What does this case tell us?
Or
What can we learn from this case?

➢ 大自然给我们的启示
What Mother Nature is trying to tell us
Or
The message we get from Mother Nature

➢ 公共图书馆转型给我们的启示
What transformation of public libraries tells us
Or
The implication of transformation of public libraries

➢ 此次政治大地震给我们带来的启示
What this past political earthquake has told us
Or
The implication of this past political earthquake
Or
What this past political earthquake has revealed to us

企业 (qi ye): *business* or *enterprise*

Two misconceptions to break: first, as an organization, an *enterprise* in not necessarily bigger than a *business*; second, *enterprise* is not a formal version of *business*.

While *business* is a general term for 企业 (in addition to 生意, 买卖), there is a fine distinction between *business* and *enterprise*.

Generally, *business* refers to traditional businesses, those we have come to know for generations, from the mom-and-pop stores to the Ford Motor Company. *Enterprise* is often reserved for businesses that are unconventional and risky, such as the start-up companies.

Entrepreneurs are those who dare to take risks in investing in a business. *Businessmen* are those who do buying and selling.

So 中国企业家俱乐部 has its official English name, *China Entrepreneur Club*, suggesting that its members include those daring, adventurous businesspersons who founded many firsts in China.

Hence, 创业精神 is translated to *entrepreneurship*, never *business spirit*.

When 企业 refers to operation, not the structure or type of ownership (e.g., company, corporation, firm, etc.), we see

➤ 企业管理 *business management*
➤ 企业竞争模拟 *business competition simulation*
➤ 企业经营 *business operation*
➤ 企业战略 *business strategy*
➤ 企业规模 *business scope*
➤ 私营企业 *private enterprise* or *private business*
➤ 国营企业 *state enterprise, government-owned enterprise, state-owned business, government-owned business.*

R

人才 (ren cai): *talent* or *professionals*

Granted, the term 人才 is a big word, and one often hears in the news that companies are coming up with all sorts of ways to retain talent. Many companies have a talent acquisition division.

But not every 人才 needs to be translated as *talent*. In some cases, the term 人才 is used just to add a touch of courtesy to the person in question. It is often used in a much looser way to mean anyone with a skill or two.

Decades ago in China, a bus driver was a 人才.

Examples:

> 国军人才招募中心
> Recruitment center of the National Armed Forces

> AOL 在激烈的市场竞争中, 努力留住人才。
> AOL tried to retain talent in the heated competition for market shares,

> 为了避免人才外流, 政府推出一系列优惠政策。
> To prevent brain drain, the government has unveiled a host of favorable policies.

> 我们为公司提供人才招聘服务
> We provide companies with a recruitment service.

> 我们公司需要大批翻译人才
> My company needs a large number of linguists.

➤ 尽快招聘并储备合适人才，以备日后市场开拓。
Quickly recruit and reserve qualified personnel for future market expansion.

认真 (ren zhen): *serious, earnest,* or *sincere*

认真 has two meanings: one is about attitude—*serious, earnest, sincere, diligent,* and so forth; the other is about procedure—*detailed, thorough, careful,* and so forth.

What is the difference? Well, the first three sentences below are about attitude, *serious/seriously* is correctly used for 认真, but 认真 in the last four sentences is more about procedure. If treated as attitude, then it is a very low standard.

认真to describe attitude:

➤ 别笑! 认真点! 这是个生命关天的大事。
Stop laughing! Be serious! This is a matter of life or death.

➤ 她工作很认真, 从来不吊儿郎当的。
She is serious with her work and never fools around.

➤ 他认真对待学生的每一个问题
He takes every question from students seriously.

认真to describe procedure:

➤ 教师要认真检查考题, 以防有误。
Teachers should carefully check test questions to avoid errors.
(Check test questions *seriously/sincerely*? Does it suggest teachers are otherwise not serious?)

> 行销部门要认真准备市场报告, 为下次董事会作准备。
> The marketing department should prepare detailed market reports to get things ready for the board meeting.
> (Prepare reports *seriously/sincerely*? What is it trying to say? Are people not serious otherwise?)

> 管理层要认真分析当前形势
> The management should make a thorough analysis of current situations.
> (Again, using any of the three attitude words—*seriously, sincerely, diligently*—would suggest that we ask the managers to take their work seriously this time. Isn't that too low a standard?)

> 管理人员在分析市场动态时, 要认真仔细。
> Managers should pay close attention to details when analyzing market situations.
> (Likewise, 认真 here is more about the action—*pay attention to details*, not *attitude*. Otherwise, it would be like expecting a chef not to goof around in the kitchen.)

S

社会 (she hui): *social* or *societal*

As used in 社会影响, 社会因素, 社会问题. One often sees social/societal influence, social/societal factors, or social/societal issues.

While some readers find *societal* pretentious, others insist that *societal* expresses what *social* doesn't.

Here is the distinction. *Social* is about the components of society: people, families, organizations, and so forth. *Societal* is about society as a whole versus other societies in an international context.

When translating 社会因素 as *social factors*, the linguist is looking at the factors of the components of society: people, families, organizations, and so forth. When translating 社会因素 as *societal factors*, the linguist is looking at the society as a whole against the backdrop of other societies.

For example, in the context of an international agreement on, say, forest conservation, some nations argue that forests should be preserved to protect the environment, while others want to cut down trees for more farmland.

The influence of these societies constitutes *societal factors* (社会因素), which must be taken into account in order to reach an agreement. But leaders of these nations are facing *social pressure* (社会压力) when they talk to their people about the issue.

Simply put, *social* expresses interactions among people within a society; *societal* is about interactions among societies of different nations.

Societal is not a formal version of *social*, nor is *societal* a flowery expression in place of *social*.

申请 (shen qing): *apply* or *request*

Dictionaries define *apply* as *make a formal request*. Not much help.

But in real-life usage, one would find a fine distinction, which helps us know when to use *apply* (申请) and when to use *request* (more like 请求).

In general, *apply* involves application for school admission, job, scholarship, membership, and the like; *request* involves favors, help, demand, and the like.

Examples:

> 申请成为该组织的会员
> Apply for membership of this organization.

> 申请资助
> Apply for financial support.

> 申请签证
> Apply for a visa.

> 申请放行
> Request clearance.

> 申请举手表决
> Request a decision by a show of hands.

> 人手不够时, 可提出申请, 我给你派几个人来。
> When you are short of hands, you can submit a request, and I will send some people over.

> 需要新设备的部门, 要在十日内提出书面申请。
> The departments that need new equipment should submit a written request within ten days.

是 (shi): *to be* or *not to be*

It seems to be the easiest Chinese word to translate, but watch out! The Chinese language uses 是 differently from its English cousin *be*.

是 is rendered as *be* only in the context of 我是学生; 米是粮食; 梨是水果, or as a linking verb, to use a grammar term; namely, linking 我 with 学生; 米 with 粮食; 梨 with 水果.

But it is utterly wrong to use the *be* verb in the following cases:

➢ 图1是市场变化曲线
Figure 1 shows the curve of a market change.
(A figure is not a curve; it is only a diagram. A line can be a curve.)

➢ 表1 是每台电脑的价格
Table 1 shows the price for each computer.
(A table is not a price; it only shows the price.)

➢ 左边图表是目前公司的状况
The diagram on the left illustrates the current status of the company.
(A diagram is not a status; it only shows the status.)

➢ 这个方法是将两组人员合并为一
This method combines the two groups of people into one.
Or
What this method does is combine the two groups of people into one.
(A method is not a combination; it is an approach.)

➢ 集中控制是将所有控制权集中在一个部门。
Centralized control refers to the concentration of all control power in one office.
Or
Centralized control means that all control power is concentrated in one office.

Or

By centralized control, it is meant that all control power is exercised by one office.

属于(shu yu): *belong to* or not

Belong to may readily come to mind to translate 属于, but in some cases, 属于 simply functions as 是, the simple linking verb *to be*.

Examples:

➤ 这条街上有许多商店, 其中一家属私营商店。

There are many stores on this street, and one of them is a private business.

(Here, the message is about the nature of the ownership of a particular store: state owned or privately owned. If translated as *belongs to a privately owned store*, it could be misleading to mean that this particular store is the property of another private business.)

➤ 这个城市有六个机场, 其中三个属一级机场。

This city has six airports, three of them being a Class I airport.

(*Belongs to a Class I airport* could suggest that these three airports are under the jurisdiction of the other three Class I airports. But this is not the message. Like the one above, it suggests the class of the three airports.)

➤ 这个地区属亚热带气候。

This region is in a subtropical climate.

(*Belongs to a subtropical climate* would sound weird; climate doesn't own the region.)

➢ 他是属于紧张型的那种。

He is the nervous type.

➢ 这个公司属于合资企业。

This company falls under the category of a joint venture.

Or

This company is a joint venture.

➢ 他的观点纯属垃圾!

His remarks belong in trash!

His opinions are rubbish!

速度 (su du): *speed* or *velocity*

Granted, the two are all about how fast an object moves, but they are different in a very subtle and important aspect.

Strictly speaking, *speed* and *velocity* are not interchangeable, nor is *velocity* the formal version of *speed*. Not at all. In physics, *velocity* is 速度, and *speed* is 速率.

To non-technical readers on non-technical subjects, using one for the other may not cause serious miscommunication, and *speed* can take care of most of 速度.

But to technology-savvy readers, such a misuse often spells embarrassment on the part of the linguist.

Speed is all about how fast an object moves, not so much about where it is going.

A good example is a moving car. For a physicist, if a car is traveling 100 miles an hour, regardless of where the car is going, he is seeing a speed of 100 mph. To translate 速度 in this context, a physicist reader would expect *speed*.

Velocity, on the other hand, is about both speed and direction.

For the same physicist reader, if a car is running 100 miles an hour to a destination, he is seeing *velocity*. 速度 in this context should be translated to *velocity*.

In other words, *speed* is a scalar quantity not interested in direction; *velocity* is a vector quantity interested in direction. To a physicist, a racing car traveling in circles on a race track may have a high *speed*, but it has no *velocity*.

Simply put, when 速度 appears in an everyday context, such as wind blowing, driving a car, jogging, walking on a treadmill, water running, eating a meal, and the like, where direction is not in the picture, one can safely translate 速度 as *speed*.

But when 速度 appears in a technical subject, such as launching missiles or rockets, playing baseball, and the like, where direction is very much part of the equation, one can safely translate 速度 as *velocity*.

Let us take a look at how 速度 should be translated in real-life situations.

> 好的棒球投手能投出每小时100英里的速度
> A good pitcher can throw a baseball at a velocity of 100 mph.
> (You would find *speed* used sometimes in this context, but to satisfy word-savvy readers, *velocity* is a better choice.)

> 导弹高速地飞向目标
> The missile flew to the target at a high velocity.
> (The missile is flying to a target. A direction is in the equation.)

> 货币流通速度
> Velocity of circulation of money

Or

Transaction velocity of money

Or

> Velocity of money
> (It is about how fast, say, one dollar is circulated in the market in a given time. A direction is involved—from consumer to merchandise, back to consumer, and back to merchandise, and so forth.)

➤ 这款车速在每小时65 哩时, 引擎运转最好。
This car engine runs best at a speed of 65 mph.
(It is not about how far it covers in a given time, nor is it about where it goes. Rather, it is simply about how many revolutions the engine makes in a given time. The car may be stationary, with the engine running.)

➤ 高速导弹
High-velocity missile
(It is about how far it can travel in a given time before it hits its target, Both displacement and target are in the equation.)

➤ 高速相机
High-speed camera
(It is about how fast the shutter can click; no distance is involved.)

➤ 高速英特网接入
High-speed Internet access
(Again, it is about how fast one can get connected to the Internet; no distance is involved.)

T

条件 (tiao jian): *condition* or something else

Like many other Chinese words, 条件 is readily translated as *condition* in dictionaries, but not every 条件 should be rendered as *condition*.

In different contexts, it can be *criterion*, *qualification*, or *credential*, among many others. 条件 in these cases is more like 资格.

Examples:

➢ 评委们定出了几项评选条件, 供评选时参考。
The judges have put forth several selection criteria as a reference when making decisions.
(*Selection conditions* would be vague. Does it mean conditions the panel has to meet before they make their decision?)

➢ 是否让他担任这个职务要看他的政治条件
Whether or not he is given this position depends on his political qualifications.

➢ 现在研发这个系统的条件尚不成熟
The conditions for developing this system are not ripe yet.

➢ 让你去, 你还不够条件。
You are not qualified to go.

➢ 申报 "千人计划" 的人选应具有下列条件。
Applicants to the "1000 Talents" program should demonstrate the following credentials.

➢ 他还不具备独当一面的条件。
He is not ready yet to take charge.

➢ 政府对条件困难的家庭给与补助。
Government provides subsidies to poor families.

➢ 我看你们俩的条件不错, 就结婚吧!
It looks like you two are a good match. Why don't you get married?

同情 (tong qing): *sympathy* or *empathy*

This is another case where dictionaries give both *sympathy* and *empathy* for 同情. While they both express feelings for the sad news of others, they each carry a different emotional message.

Sympathy expresses sharing sad feelings, feeling sorry for others; *empathy* not only expresses the same compassion but also tells others, "I feel your pain because I was once in the same shoes."

Sympathy can be an understanding on a rational level—I understand your pain; things will get better sooner or later.

Empathy is an understanding on a personal level—I understand your pain because I have been through the same experience.

Next time, when you come across 同情, try to see which level of compassion it expresses.

Context may give a hint to when 同情 is *empathy* and when it's *sympathy*.

When a cancer support group expresses 同情 with a member's pain during radiation therapy, most likely its 同情 is *empathy*. Reason: members of the group are also patients, and they know firsthand how it feels.

When a male doctor expresses his 同情 with a pregnant woman's discomfort during her delivery, his 同情 is *sympathy*. Reason: he can only understand it but never feels it.

Examples:

➤ 在我困难的时候, 你们的同情让我很感动。
I was touched by your sympathy during my difficult time.

➤ 我们不仅要同情穷人, 还应帮他们改善处境。
Not only should we sympathize with the poor, but we also should help them to improve their conditions.
(We feel sorry for the poor, but we may never have been poor.)

Or

Not only should we empathize with the poor, but we also should help them improve their conditions.
(We were once poor just like them, so we know what it feels like to be poor.)

➤ 我们都看到了她对那个求救的孩子所表现的同情
We all could clearly see her empathy for the child crying for help.
(She must have had a similar experience to that of the child.)

Or

We all could clearly see her sympathy for the child crying for help.
(She feels sad, but she may not have experienced what the child is experiencing.)

➤ 政府对煤矿遇难工人的家属深表同情
The government expresses deep sympathy for the families of the workers who died in the coal mine accident.

(*Empathy* should not be used here, as government is an organization, an abstract concept, impossible to experience coal mine accidents or the like.)

The following sentence gives a better picture of what *sympathy* and *empathy* each mean:

> ➤ The media must not mistake the empathy we feel for the victim with sympathy for his views.
> 媒体不应把我们对死者的同情误认为是对他的观点的认同

统一 (tong yi): *uniform* or *unified*

统一, as an adjective, is one of the most frequently used terms in official Chinese communication. It looks harmless until one is faced with the tough choice: *uniform* or *unified*, both under 统一.

Simply put, *unified* often is followed by words that suggest human efforts (leadership, management, approach, strategy, command, communication, action, and the like).

Uniform often is followed by words that suggest objects (price, speed, sign, color, layout, standard, design, and so forth).

When one sees, "The court advocates a unified standard of procedure review," one may read, "Joint efforts are needed to establish a standard."

When one sees, "The court advocates a uniform standard of procedure review," one may read, "There is one standard to dictate all procedures."

So in 保持统一步伐, the term 步伐, although a noun, clearly suggests the effort to do the same thing, not the physical steps; therefore, it is appropriate to say "maintain a unified effort/action."

In 配戴统一帽盔, the term 帽盔, also a noun, hardly suggests efforts. It is an object on one's head, so it is best to say, "wear uniform helmets."

Examples:

> 这是公司制定的统一零售价, 不会有二价。
> This is the uniform retail price set by the company, and there shall be no other prices.

> 国际标准可以在世界范围内统一使用
> International standards can be used uniformly all over the world.

> 在党的统一领导下
> Under the unified leadership of the Party

> 应该有个统一时间表
> There should be a uniform schedule.

> 停车场服务人员要求佩戴统一标志
> Badges should be uniform for parking lot personnel.

> 明天的会, 我们要做统一安排。
> We need a unified arrangement for tomorrow's conference.

Or

We need to make an arrangement in a unified manner.
(All parties put their heads together to work out a plan.)

> 采取统一行动
> Take unified action.

> 年终工作讲评, 要有一个统一标准。
> There should be a uniform standard for year-end performance evaluation.

W

外交 (wai jiao): *diplomacy, foreign affairs,* or *foreign service*

Dictionaries can easily scoop up all three English terms under 外交, but that often leaves translators scratching their heads. Is it *diplomacy, foreign affairs,* or *foreign service* for 外交?

Diplomacy is about skills in doing 外交. Its Chinese variant is 外交手段, 外交途径. *Foreign affairs* is about the content of 外交. Its Chinese variant is 外交事务. *Foreign service* is about the profession, the job. Its Chinese variant is 外交工作.

Now, more about 外交, translated as *diplomacy*. It is not the profession of foreign service. It is how people do the job—negotiation, personal charm, compromise, smiles, tears, persuasion, and even threats.

It is about the skills. It is the tool.

So, as a tool, we have these many 外交:

➢ *public diplomacy* (公共外交)
➢ *prudent diplomacy* (谨慎外交)
➢ *Beijing diplomacy* (北京外交)
➢ *handshake diplomacy* (握手外交)
➢ *dollar diplomacy* (美元外交)
➢ *ping-pong diplomacy* (乒乓外交)
➢ *smile diplomacy* (微笑外交)
➢ *carrot-and-stick diplomacy* (胡萝卜加大棒外交)
➢ *panda diplomacy* (熊猫外交)
➢ *gourmet diplomacy* (美食外交)

The list can go on and on.

Without exception, they are *not* about the job (外交工作) but about how people go about doing the job, resolving issues between nations, and using smiles or ping-pong balls or good food.

With these differences spelled out, let's see how we translate the following 外交phrases:

➤ 我校相当一部分学生毕业后, 从事外交。
   Quite a number of students, upon graduation, went to work in foreign service (or joined the diplomatic corps or became a diplomat). (They didn't work in *diplomacy* because 外交 here refers to a job, not the approach and skills. Otherwise, *work in diplomacy* would be 从事外交手段. Awkward, isn't it?)

➤ 领土争端要通过外交解决
   Territorial disputes should be resolved through diplomacy
   (It is not *foreign service* because 外交 does not refer to a job but how disputes should be resolved—war or negotiation.)

➤ 外交无小事
   Nothing is too small in foreign affairs.
Or
   Foreign service is a serious business.
   (外交, in this context, is about the profession (*foreign service*) and world affairs (*foreign affairs*). But it should not be *diplomacy*. It is not talking about the skill.)

➤ 外交在很大程度上就是公共外交
   Diplomacy, to a large extent, is all about public diplomacy.
   (外交, in this context, is about the approach to resolving issues. It is not about foreign service as a job, or about foreign affairs as events.)

➤ 这在外交界已不是秘密了
   This is no longer a secret in the diplomatic community.

卫生 (wei sheng): *sanitation, health,* or something else

This is one of those terms that has multiple meanings. One has to double-check the context in which it is used for an appropriate rendition.

Examples:

➤ 卫生部门
Health departments/agencies

➤ 居民楼的供暖, 消防和卫生要达标。
Residential buildings should meet the requirements for heating, fire prevention, and sanitation.

➤ 这里的卫生条件很好, 不用担心生病。
It is very clean here. You don't have to worry about getting sick.

➤ 部队的卫生员主要留在了后方
Most of the medics stayed in the rear.

➤ 夏天饮食要注意卫生
In summer, one must make sure that drinks and food are clean.

➤ 学校要教孩子们注意个人卫生。
The school must teach children about personal hygiene.

➤ 今天打扫卫生。
We will do general cleaning today.

文化 (wen hua): *culture* or something else

In Chinese, the word 文化 (*culture*) can mean those grandiose subjects, such as religion, politics, language, art, and so forth, but it also can mean schooling or entertainment activities.

Examples:

➤ 他的文化水平不高
He does not have much education.

➤ 旅途中, 列车乘客需要丰富的文化生活。
Passengers need a great variety of entertainment while on the train.

➤ 过去, 政府号召人人学文化。
In the past, the government encouraged the public to learn to read and write.

➤ 招募员工时, 要看一个人的文化背景。
When hiring people, one's education is something to be taken into account.

➤ 他很有文化
He is well educated.

文明 (wen ming): *civilized* or something else

Civilized is often the choice for 文明, as in 文明单位, 文明服务, but it is a bad choice.

Civilized is mostly associated with the sense of not being savage, barbarous, or inhumane, as in its Chinese equivalent of 不野蛮, 不凶残, 人道.

Is文明 (as in文明单位, 文明服务) trying to say 不野蛮单位, 不野蛮服务? I don't think so. It is like a shop clerk saying "We won't rob you" to customers.

See the awkward result?

Examples:

➢ 家家争作文明家庭

All families are striving to be model families.

(It simply means *good families*. To say *civilized families* would suggest there will not be violence—no killing, no barbarous behavior. Isn't that too low a standard?)

➢ 文明服务是我店的宗旨

Excellent service is the goal of our store.

(To say *civilized service* would be saying that the store would not treat you rudely. Not a desirable goal.)

➢ 这是京津线的文明列车

This is the train with the best customer service on the Beijing-Tianjin line.

(What is a *civilized train* like? Passengers behave themselves—no cursing, no drunkards, no fighting, no killing.)

➢ 本站连续两年被评为文明车站

This station has been awarded Outstanding Station two years in a row.

(*Civilized station* would paint the same picture—no savage people. No fighting for seats. No killing for train tickets, if they need tickets to begin with.)

➢ 文明经商

Do business by the rules.

(If translated as "Do business in a civilized way," does it mean no cursing, no screaming, no short-changing, no shoving customers out of the store? Or is this what they used to do, and now they want to behave a little better?)

➢ 他为人处事文明礼貌。

He conducts himself with civility.

Or

He is thoughtful and polite.

(He is *civilized* and *courteous*. My God! People around him must be savage and rude.)

稳定 (wen ding): *stable* or *steady*

Although both *stable* and *steady* appear under 稳定, they are not absolutely synonymous. One can still see a subtle distinction.

While *stable* expresses the idea of 稳定 as a state of being, *steady* does it as a manner of action. In other words, *stable* is often followed by a "state" noun, denoting a standstill, static situation, more like 固定, but *steady* is often followed by an "action" noun, suggesting an ongoing activity, more like 稳步, 平稳.

Examples:

➢ 稳定的收入

Stable income

(A set monthly income; can be translated back to 固定收入)

Or

Steady income

(A set monthly income coming your way, consistently)

The following collocation shows where *stable* and *steady* are each often used.

Stable:

- ✓ Stable condition
- ✓ Stable desk
- ✓ Stable job
- ✓ Stable mood
- ✓ Stable object
- ✓ Stable relationship
- ✓ Stable situation
- ✓ Stable size

Steady:

- ✓ Steady blow
- ✓ Steady breeze
- ✓ Steady decline in birth rate
- ✓ Steady development
- ✓ Steady flow of water
- ✓ Steady hand (not shaking or trembling)
- ✓ Steady influx of refugees
- ✓ Steady ladder (firmly placed, not wobbling)
- ✓ Steady progress
- ✓ Steady speed

Most of *stable* and *steady* above may be 稳定 in Chinese, but whether it denotes action (speed, progress) or state (situation, condition) is critical.

问题 (wen ti): *problem* or *issue*

This is another case where 问题 has two translations: *problem* and *issue* (*question* should not be an issue). But they are not an absolute synonym.

Here is the difference in a broad stroke. Translate 问题 to *problem,* when 问题 suggests something needs a solution—a clear-cut one, like a math problem. There is no room for debate or compromise.

Translate 问题 to *issue,* when 问题 suggests something involves discussion, debate, controversy, or conflict of ideas. There is no clear-cut right or wrong.

Poverty is a social *problem*, but homosexuality is a social *issue.*

There is no debate about whether poverty is right or wrong, so it is a *problem.*

Homosexuality is a personal preference, a matter of different opinions. So it is an *issue.*

Poverty—a *problem*—involves no conflict of ideas. Everybody agrees to put an end to poverty.

Homosexuality—an *issue*—concerns different opinions. Some think it's right, while others don't approve of it.

问题, as a *problem,* must be remedied; 问题, as an *issue,* doesn't have to be put to rights. It can reemerge as a different form of an issue, as a result of compromise.

Another tip to use *problem* and *issue* correctly: when translating 解决问题, we *resolve* an issue, but we *solve* a problem.

Resolution (verb: resolve) explains and works around conflicting ideas (homosexuality). Thus, we *resolve issues.* Solution (verb: solve) finds a clear-cut end to a problem (poverty). Thus, we *solve problems.*

Examples:

➢ 我们先把加薪的问题放一放, 集中讨论公司偷税漏税的问题。
Let's set aside the pay raise issue and focus on the company's problem of tax evasion.
(This assumes a lot of negotiation goes into who gets a raise and how much—an issue; but tax evasion is flatly wrong—a problem.)

➢ 一个公司总是有一大堆资金问题, 比如现金流动, 律师费用, 市场扩展, 员工福利, 如此等等。
A company is never short of financial issues, such as cash flow, legal expenses, market expansion, employees' benefits, and so forth.
(These 问题 are not troubles to be remedied; they are the concerns to be addressed. Cash is still flowing but in a more acceptable way.)

➢ 我们之间存在的问题不是几句话就能解决的
The issues between us cannot be resolved in a few words.
(This assumes these are not flatly right or wrong 问题, like squeezing the toothpaste tube from the bottom or from the middle.)

➢ 我们之间存在的问题不是几句话就能解决的
The problems between us cannot be solved in a few words.
(This assumes these 问题 involve stealing and telling lies. It is a matter of right or wrong and must be set right.)

X

新 (xin): *new* or *novel*

Most likely, the choice is *new*. Nothing wrong with that, but some may choose to use *novel*.

A word of caution: *novel* is not a formal version of *new*.

While they both translate as 新, they each express a different layer of nuance. *New* is about something recent in time, different from the old, latest in a sequence. *Novel* is about something unusual, creative, unique, striking, or original.

Simply put, *new* is more about "recent"; it doesn't have to be unique. *Novel* is more about "unique"; it doesn't have to be recent.

Examples:

➤ 新一代领导人
A new generation of leadership

➤ 新问题
A new problem

➤ 新朋友
New friends

➤ 新车
A new car

➤ 新年
New Year

We say *new*, not *novel*, for the above 新 because they are built on the conventional understanding that 新 is a time concept, a value relative to old. It has nothing to do with being striking, unique, creative, or the one and only.

However, the following 新 can go both ways:

➤ 新技术

A novel technology—a creation; an invention; no one else has it.

Or

A new technology—there was an old one, but this one has come along lately.

➤ 新方法

A novel approach—a unique method.

Or

A new approach—maybe a second attempt with a different method.

➤ 新想法

A novel idea—an unusual concept; original; no one else has it.

Or

A new idea—a new concept heard recently; different from old-fashioned ones.

➤ 新产品

A novel product—a creation; an invention; an unusual product.

Or

A new product—something produced lately.

性 (xing): as a suffix (not *sex*—sorry)

As used in 科学性, 娱乐性, 实用性.

It is one of the most freely used words in the Chinese language and the most difficult to translate too.

In Chinese, by adding the suffix 性 to a noun, an adjective, or a verb, it simply suggests that something has a particular quality.

The English language does not have such a one-size-fits-all suffix, other than the suffix "-ty" in *creativity* 创造性, *continuity* 连续性, *reliability* 可靠性, *flexibility* or *agility* 灵活性; or the "-ness" in *aggressiveness* 好斗性, *forgetfulness* 健忘性, *laziness* 懒惰性, *truthfulness* 真实性, just to name a few.

To deal with these 性 expressions in Chinese, you must work around them. Often, a simple adjective may do the trick.

Examples:

➢ 吃五谷杂粮对感冒具有抵抗性
Including a great variety of grains in your diet can help protect against the common flu.

➢ 他的话极具煽动性
His remarks are extremely provocative.

➢ 挑逗性言语
Suggestive remarks

➢ 政治性极强的事件
Highly politically-charged events
Or
Highly political events

> 政策性亏损
>
> Policy-related loss

> 我们政策的科学性
>
> The science behind our policy

Or

> The scientism of our policy

Or

> There is science in our policy.

> 这是一个具有革命性的建议
>
> This is a revolutionary suggestion.

> 这本书可读性不强
>
> This book is not much fun to read.

Or

> This book is not easy reading.

> 这是一项极具挑战性的工作
>
> This is an extremely challenging job.

研究 (yan jiu): *research* or *study*

研究 is translated as both *research* and *study*.

While the two can cover 研究 most of the time, *research* and *study* each express a different type of 研究, in a subtle way.

While *research* is more about collecting data, *study* says more about making sense of the data collected.

Research is more about *what*; *study* more about *why*.

In other words, *research* is about finding data; *study* is about making sense of the data found

In other words, when 研究 is about 调研, 调查, 查考, 查找, 探寻, *research* is the word choice. When 研究is about 分析, 研判, 探究, 研读, *study* is the word choice.

Here is a good example. A **USA Today** article (July 13, 2016) cites Congresswomen Blackburn as saying that the Clinton Foundation claims to engage in study and research in its filings with the IRS.

Note the use of *study* and *research* in one breath.

What the foundation does is conduct research (collect data) and study (make sense of the data collected).

Research presents *what*; *study* explains *why*.

Examples:

> 多少年来, 心理学家们一直在探究人们说谎的原因。研究表明, 人们说谎是出于各种各样的原因。

For decades, psychologists have been researching why people cheat. Their studies show that people often are pulled by multiple reasons to cheat.

(探究*research*: find the reasons; 研究 *study*: explain the reasons found.)

> 一位美国高中生赢得头等奖, 因为她的研究发现能精确找到癌症肿瘤的方法。据信, 大约还需要25年左右的时间, 她的研究成果才能用于治疗病人。

A high school student from the USA won a top prize for her research that found ways to target cancer tumors with precision. It is believed that it could take about twenty-five years before her research can help patients.

(研究 *research*: find precision ways to target cancer tumors.)

> 通过研究它们之间的异同，我们发现，它们属同一种植物。
>
> Through studying their differences and similarities, we found that they belong to the same kind of plant.
>
> (研究 *study*: explain the differences and similarities.)

> 我们要广泛研究古今中外案例
>
> We should research widely into cases ancient and current, Chinese and foreign.
>
> (研究 *research*: collect information of such cases and make sense of them.)

Or

> We should study various cases ancient and current, Chinese and foreign.
>
> (研究 *study*: analyze, make sense of information collected of such cases.)

> 学生每学期要交两份研究报告
>
> Students must turn in two research papers each semester.
>
> (研究 *research*: find information to support a theme.)

> 研究结果表明家中过滤水比瓶装水干净
>
> Research findings show that filtered tap water is cleaner than bottled water.
>
> (研究 *research*: collect data to support the argument.)

> 美国研究所有很多研究项目。
>
> The Institute of American Studies hosts many research projects.
>
> (研究 *studies*: understand, make sense of the country.)

> 刚才出了一个大事故，咱们马上开会研究对策。
>
> There was a serious accident just now. Let's meet right away to find a solution.

(It would give a wrong picture to say *study a solution*, as if a solution already existed to be examined.)

> 破译专家被招来逐字研究此文件
> Cryptographers are called in to study this document word by word.
> (研究 *study*: examine and make sense of the words.)

> 在此方案公布前, 你们还要就它的可行性作一番研究。
> You should do some research into its feasibility before the plan is released.
> (研究 *research*: find out whether the plan can be carried out.)

> 此方案的可行性报告我们研究过了, 认为它没有考虑到未来两年的物价飙升问题。
> We have studied the feasibility report of this plan, only to conclude that it fails to take into account the price hike in the next two years.
> (研究 *study*: make sense of the report, with the data collection completed.)

Of course, 研究 can render many other expressions in everyday situations, such as:

> 你的情况我们得先研究研究再给你答复。
> We will review your case before we give you an answer.

> 领导会仔细研究一下你的建议的。
> The management will look into your suggestions.

> 经过再三研究, 我们决定给你加薪。
> After a careful review, we have decided to give you a raise.

> 这样吧, 我们研究研究再说。
> Well, we will give it some thought first and get back to you.

Y

验证 (yan zheng): *verify* or *validate*

Which one to use? They both mean to prove something to be true. In most cases, these two are used interchangeably, but in certain situations, one has to make a choice.

In computer testing and engineering, among other sectors, *verify* and *validate* differ not in meaning but in what they each are checking, or 验证.

Simply put, *verify* is to 验证 whether a product or system is properly engineered; *validate* is to 验证 whether the product or system meets the need of its intended user, albeit it is put together nicely.

Take a bike for example. To 验证 whether it has all the parts necessary to be a bike, one needs to see it has two pedals, chain, brakes, wheels, seat, and so forth. This 验证 is *verify*.

But to 验证 whether a bike, which has all the necessary parts, is for its intended user—small kid, big kid, adult, or athlete, one needs to check the bike size and gadgets. This 验证 is *validate*.

Take a hospital parking ticket, for example. When the parking lot attendant验证the parking ticket, all he/she needs to do is to see if it is a true parking ticket (not a movie ticket). He is *verifying* the ticket.

But, when the attendant 验证 the ticket to see whether the ticket holder is the intended user, namely a hospital patient or visitor (not a customer of a shopping mall across the street), the attendant is *validating* the ticket.

In this case, not only does the attendant need to see the parking ticket (make sure it is not a movie ticket), but he/she also needs to see the authorization on the ticket (a stamp from the hospital's front desk).

This is true with many government facilities, restaurants, special events, and the like.

Next time, when translating 验证 in these cases, make sure whether the guard needs to check only the ticket (*verify*, in this case), or if he/she needs to check your ID or some kind of authorization as well, to make sure you are the right person (*validate*, in this case).

Validate is asking, "Are you building the product for the right user?"; namely, a product that meets the needs of the user. *Verify* is asking, "Are you building the product right?"; namely, a product that is put together correctly.

In the bike example above, *validation* asks, "Are you building a children's bike or a mountain bike?" It is interested in meeting the user's need.

Verification asks. "Are you building a bike or a wheelbarrow?" It is interested in the engineering of the product.

Examples:

> When my iPhone is uploading its new operation system iOS 9.2, a message "Verifying update" shows on the screen.

   It is saying that I am checking it is the correct update—iOS 9.2—that is being uploaded. This 验证 is *verify*.

> The US Citizenship and Immigration Services has an e-verify system that allows businesses to determine the eligibility of their employees to work in the United States.

   In this case, it is 验证 in two senses: *verify* (it is the right person on the ID card) and *validate* (not only is it the right person on the ID card, but also it is the person authorized to work).

➢ On *NPR News* (5/29/2013), when reporting on the case of Liberty Reserve, Kara Scannell, US regulatory correspondent with the *Financial Times*, said, "In these online virtual currency businesses, they don't verify or validate—or at least Liberty Reserve didn't verify or validate—any of the information of its customers."

➢ 验证密码
Verify your password.
(What this 验证 asks is for the user to retype the password. It doesn't care whether it is typed by the right person or not. This would take another system to *validate*.)

影响 (ying xiang): *influence* or *affect*

Again, dictionaries list both *influence* and *affect* all under 影响. Not much help there.

But they 影响 in different ways: *influence* wants someone/something to go the influence inserter's way; *affect* wants to move someone/something away from an intended goal.

In other words, translate 影响 as *influence* when it means to manipulate someone to do things or something to happen in a certain way. Translate 影响 as *affect* when it means the intended outcome is twisted.

The working of a magnetic compass can best illustrate the point.

We say, the needle of a magnetic compass points to true north under the *influence* of the earth's magnetic field. But its equilibrium orientation also can be *affected* by the presence of a piece of metal nearby.

Both *influence* and *affected* above are 影响, but *influence* wants the compass needle to go the earth's magnetic way, pointing to true north, influencing it the inserter's way. *Affected* wants to move the needle away from the influence of the inserter's way—the intended way, pointing away from its intended true north.

One more example:

We can say, "Concerned over foreign *influence affecting* their neutrality in making decisions, the committee decided to bar its members from any contact with foreigners."

Again, both *influence* and *affecting* above are 影响, but *influence* is saying that foreigners want the members to make decisions in the foreigners' way. *Affecting* is saying that the members may cast their votes differently from their intended way—neutrality.

Examples:

➤ 受我哥哥的影响, 我也抽烟了, 结果我的血压也受到很大影响。
Under the influence of my brother, I started to smoke. As a result, it affected my blood pressure, big time.
(*Influence* is about me going my brother's way (the influence inserter's way); *affected* is about the change of my blood pressure from its intended level.)

➤ 人与人相互影响, 不是你影响他, 就是他影响你。
People influence each other, be it you influencing him, or he you.
(Here, 影响 means the influencer wants you to do things his way.)

➤ 冷天气会对樱花又很大的影响
Cold weather could seriously affect the cherry blossoms.
(Here, the 影响 is about a change from the trees' intended budding time.)

129

➢ 在措辞上一个小小的改动能影响谈判的成败
A slight change in the wording can affect the outcome of a negotiation.
(The 影响 is about a change from the intended outcome.)

➢ 不能让他的态度影响工作
We should not let his attitude affect our performance.
(The 影响 is about a change from the intended work performance.)

➢ 他想用他的权力影响团队其他成员
He wanted to use his power to influence the rest of the team.
(The 影响 is about his gearing the team to go his way, the influence inserter's way.)

➢ 公司在行业中的影响飞速增长
The company's influence in the industry is growing rapidly.
(The 影响 is about the power the influence inserter—the company—to make others follow its footsteps.)

➢ 酒精影响了他的判断力
Alcohol affects his ability to make judgments.
(The 影响 is about a change from his normal judgment ability.)

➢ 我不想影响他们做决定
I don't want to influence their decision making.
(The 影响 is about the power to persuade them to make a decision.)

➢ 我的话影响了他们的决定
My remarks affected their decision.
(Here, 影响 is about the result of their decision, a change from their intended decision.)

勇敢 (yong gan): *courageous* or *brave*

As an adjective, both *brave* and *courageous* translate as勇敢, but as a noun, they are different in meaning. While *bravery* is 勇敢, *courage* is 勇气.

What is the difference? *Bravery* is the ability to confront danger without thinking of or feeling fear; *courage* is the ability to confront danger, knowing full well the presence of danger and feeling the fear but not being stopped by the fear.

With this difference in mind, the two 勇敢 can render differently.

明知山有虎，偏向虎山行(Heading toward the mountains, knowing full well there are tigers lurking around) is a *courageous* act.

Whereas, 听到救命声，一个行人纵身跳入湍急的河里 (Hearing the cry for help, a passer-by jumped into the rushing river) is a *brave* act.

In the tiger case, the person clearly is aware of the danger, but he moves on regardless. In the river case, the passer-by barely has a moment to think about danger.

初生牛犊不怕虎 (A newborn calf is not afraid of a tiger) is about the *bravery* of a calf. It does not run away when a tiger comes its way. It is *brave*; it has no idea what a tiger would do to him.

But the calf's mother would fight the tiger to the death. It is *courage*—she knows she is no match, but her desire to protect her baby overpowers her fear.

A soldier rushing back amid enemy fire to drag his comrade to safety can be both a *brave* and a *courageous* act.

He is *courageous*. He knows he can be killed, but he has no time to think about his life.

He is a *brave*. His act is impulsive, without thinking of or feeling fear.

In the biblical story of David and Goliath, David's 勇敢 is *brave*, not *courageous*. His triumph over Goliath is the example of *bravery*, not *courage*.

Next time, when translating勇敢, try to see whether it is *brave* or *courageous*.

用 (yong): *use, utilize,* or *adopt*

First of all, which one to use (or utilize): *use* or *utilize*? *Utilize* is often treated as, unfortunately, the formal version of *use* by some and seen as being pretentious by others.

In the first case, *utilize* is not—I repeat *not*—a formal version of *use*. They mean two different things, as shown below.

In the case of "being pretentious," if you don't want to run the risk of offending your word-savvy readers, you are better off using *use*.

Here is what is generally accepted by grammarians: *use* suggests that an object is being used for the purpose for which it is designed; *utilize* suggests that an object is used *not* for its intended purpose.

Examples:

➢ We *use* a fork to eat spaghetti (a fork is designed for this function).
➢ We *utilize* a fork to open a beer bottle (a fork is not designed as a beer-bottle opener but is used as a better-than-nothing alternative).
➢ Terrorists *utilize* fertilizer to make bombs (making bombs is not the intended purpose of fertilizer).
➢ Farmers *use* fertilizer for the crops (feeding crops is the intended purpose of fertilizer).
➢ Tom *uses* his notebook to take notes in class (a notebook is meant for note taking).

> Tom *utilizes* notebooks as a pillow to take a quick nap in the library (a notebook is not meant to serve as a pillow).
> We *use* coaxial cable to connect our TV to the antenna (a coaxial cable is intended for this purpose).
> We *utilize* paper clips to connect our TV to the antenna (paper clips are not designed for this purpose).

Now you get the picture.

To avoid offending word-savvy, pretentiousness-sensitive readers, it is better to use *utilize* when you want to suggest improvising: a fork as a beer-bottle opener; a water balloon as a pillow; a key chain as a plant hanger; a clothes hanger as a TV antenna; a wine glass as a candleholder.

In all other cases of 用, *use* works perfectly.

Now, let's talk about *adopt*.

Where *adopt* is used, often is the case when 采用 appears. The reason: 采用 sounds more formal than 用; *adopt* more formal than *use*. Cute reasoning, but it is wrong nonetheless.

First of all, *adopt* is not a formal version of *use*, unlike in Chinese, where 采用 can be taken as a formal way of saying 用. *Adopt* is more in line with 采纳 (*agree to use*). It often denotes a sense of using an existing method or idea, one that may not be originated by the user.

In Victor Hugo's *Les Misérables*, Jean Valjean adopts the alias of Monsieur Madeleine to conceal his identity, suggesting that the name Monsieur Madeleine already existed and was available for use.

Think of it this way: a method or idea has already been proposed, and you are simply taking it over and putting it to use, like reaping the harvest of someone else's labor. There is more involved than simple *use*.

For 用 in a general sense, not in using an existing method/idea, simply use *use*.

Examples:

> 经过反复思考, 我们决定采用她的建议。
> After careful consideration, we decided to adopt her idea.
> (Her idea has been put forth. It is on the table, ready to be used.)

> 学校领导采用了去年的做法
> The school leadership adopted the approach used last year.

> 室外天线应采用收放式
> Outdoor antennas should be the retractable type.

> 训练应采用一对一的方法
> Training should be conducted on a one-on-one basis.

> 本产品仿真软件采用VC⁺⁺ 6.0 开发
> The product's simulation software is developed with the VC⁺⁺ 6.0 version.

> 他们采用灵活手段开辟新市场
> They resorted to adaptive tactics to open up new markets.

Or

They adopted flexible approaches to open up new markets.

Or

They used versatile methods to open up new markets.

Next, the difference between *use* and *usage*, as a noun, when translating 用.

People often translate 用 (or 使用) as *usage,* where *use* is the correct choice.

Another misconception: usage is the formal version of use. No. It is not. These two words may overlap in meaning, but they are *not* absolute synonyms.

Simply put, *usage*, because of the suffix "-age," refers to conventions or established patterns, much like its Chinese cousin 用法, suggesting *how* something is being used, while *use* is like the Chinese, 用处, referring to *where* something is being used.

Examples:

➤ 用后请放回原处
Place it back after use.
(It is not about *how* you use it; thus, it should never be *usage*, nor should *usage* be used to make it sound formal or sophisticated.)

➤ 智能手机的普遍使用彻底改变了人们沟通的方式
The wide use of smartphones has completely changed how people communicate.
(*Usage* is not correct. It is not about an established practice or a customary manner.)

➤ 这个字的用法起源于15 世纪
The usage of this word dates back to the fifteenth century.
(*Usage* is correct! It is about how the word has been used since the fifteenth century.)

➤ 这个颜色用在这不好
The use of this color here is a bad idea.
(*Use* is correct! It is about the act of using in a given situation, not about an established or habitual practice.)

> ➤ 公司领导要不断审查公交补贴的使用情况
>
> The company management must constantly review the usage of the Public Transport Compensation.
>
> (It is about finding a pattern in using the benefit.)

> ➤ 公司领导通知, 员工要再填一张使用公交补贴的表。
>
> The company management informed employees that they need to fill out another form of Use of Public Transport Compensation.
>
> (It is about the act of using the benefit, much like using a facility or using a system.)

有效 (you xiao): *effective, efficient,* or *valid*

A simple way to use each of these words correctly is to make the following judgments:

- ✓ Use *efficient* when it is about making the most of time/effort. It is equivalent to 有效率.
- ✓ Use *effective* when it is about achieving desired effects/results. It is equivalent to 有效果.
- ✓ Use *valid* when it is about something legitimate or usable. It is equivalent to 可用.

In other words,

- ✓ 有效, as *efficient*, is often used to describe a verbal phrase (action), as in the last two examples below: 运转 (operate) and 办事 (conduct business).
- ✓ 有效, as *effective*, often describes a noun phrase (policy, idea, method, etc.).
- ✓ 有效, as *valid*, is often about authenticity, something acceptable, as in a passport or movie ticket.

To see the difference between *effective* and *valid*, one only needs to look at the respective synonyms:

- ✓ *Effective* is in the camp of *competent, workable, active, capable, productive, useful,* and *functional*.
- ✓ *Valid* is in the camp of *acceptable, accurate, true, authentic, official, real, trustworthy, genuine,* and *original*.

Next time, when you come across 有效体制, you should first ask, is it about whether the 体制 is functional (therefore, *effective*) or whether it is acceptable (therefore, *valid*)?

Examples:

➤ 他们两年前作的结论今天仍然有效。
The conclusions they made two years ago are still valid today.

➤ 乔治城大学注册办公室说, 我在天津外语学院的学分有效。
The Georgetown University Registrar's Office said that my credits at Tianjin Foreign Language Institute were valid.

➤ 政府准备推出更有效的政策以遏制通货膨胀。
The government is planning to unveil a more effective policy to rein in inflation.

➤ 这个主意很有效, 再也没有游客在这大声喧哗了。
This idea is so effective that no tourists have ever been found to talk loudly here.

➤ 这套系统运转有效, 省时省力。
This system is efficient, saving both time and effort.

> 新来的领导办事有效, 谈吐幽默。
> The new manager is efficient and humorous.

> 模拟试验验证了该方法的有效性
> Simulation tests prove the effectiveness of the method.

Z

战备 (zhan bei): *war preparedness* or *combat readiness*

Often one finds both *war preparedness* and *combat readiness* for 战备, but what is the difference, if any?

Dictionaries often don't have space to elaborate, leaving the choice at the mercy of experience and a feel for the correct usage.

Simply put, *war preparedness* refers to plans, policies, training, equipment, and troops ready to be deployed to fight a war. *Combat readiness* refers to the ability to put the preparations into action.

In other words, *preparedness* is about all resources being in place for a war. *Readiness* suggests these resources can be used at any given moment.

Preparedness may not entail combat actions, even with all resources for war ready to be deployed. *Readiness*, on the other hand, suggests combat action at any moment.

One often hears nervous doctoral students about to defend their dissertations say, "I am prepared, but I am not ready!" By this, they mean they have gone through their notes, bullet points, bibliographies, key dates and names, and so forth, but they don't want to go in there to make a presentation to the committee members.

So *war preparedness* can cover concepts such as 战备教育, 战备等级, 战备状态, 加强战备, 战备演练, 战备巡逻. They are all about preparation.

Combat readiness often can cover concepts such as 战斗准备, 随时出击, 临战状态, 来之能战. They are about going to a battle at any moment.

But be careful! There are other 战备 expressions that do not take *preparedness* and *readiness*:

➤ 战备物资 (*war materials*)
➤ 战备粮油储备 (*war food and oil reserves*)
➤ 战备公路 (*wartime highways*)
➤ 战备跑道 (*wartime runways*)
➤ 战备桥 (*wartime bridges*)

掌握 (zhang wo): *control* or not

掌握 can be translated as *control* when it means 控制/掌控, but not all 掌握 renders as control.

In other contexts, 掌握 actually means to have a clear understanding, to have a clear picture of a situation, to be on top of a situation, to know the case full well, to be kept informed, and so forth.

In the above case, 掌握 is not *control*.

Examples:

➤ 目前的情况不在我们的掌握之中。
The current situation is beyond our control.

➢ 谁能掌握明天?
Who can have tomorrow under control?

➢ 我们要掌握市场动态。
We must have a clear picture of the market.
Or
We must have a grasp of the market situation.

➢ 掌握竞争对手的情况至关重要。
Knowledge of competitors is critically important.

➢ 警方掌握了所有的证据。
The police have all the evidence.

➢ 掌握市场信息是有效决策的根本。
Being on top of the market information is the key to effective decision making.

➢ 到了70年代, 他们已掌握了制冷技术。
By the 1970s, they had already acquired the refrigeration technology.

➢ 我们先要掌握情况, 然后再说下一步。
We must get a handle on the situation before talking about our next move.

针对 (zhen dui): *target at*, *aim at* or *something else*

Like many other Chinese expressions, 针对 has forced translators to come up with translations to match it, hence *target at, aim at, direct at.*

It is a careless word-for-word translation, to say the least.

Translate these various English versions back to Chinese, and one would get 对准, 瞄准, 指向. But these are not what 针对 is saying.

In most cases, 针对 expresses the idea of 关于 (about, regarding, in terms of, with respect to, in light of, etc.).

Take a look at the following sentences, and you will find 针对is not about *target at, aim at, direct at*—not at all.

Examples:

➤ 针对你今天的表现, 我们决定你不适合再留在公司了。
  In light of what you did today, we decided you should no longer work in the company.

➤ 台湾针对大陆犯台的可能性制定其防务政策
  Taiwan builds its defense policies around a potential attack by mainland China.

➤ 针对你提的问题, 我们有以下几点解释
  In response to your questions, we have the following explanations.
Or
  To address your questions, we have the following explanations.
Or
  As far as your questions are concerned, we have the following explanations.

Or

> We have the following explanations regarding your question.

➤ 针对没有上网经验的人，我们制定了一系列计划。
For those who do not have online experience, we have made a series of plans.

➤ 针对百年罕见的旱情，村民们采取了各种方法。
The villagers were doing all they could to combat the drought that would hit the region in a century.

➤ 针对消化不良的患者，医生建议要放松心情，多多运动。。
To help those with indigestion, the doctor suggested that they should relax and exercise more.

➤ 他的这番话不是针对你的
His words were not meant for you.

➤ 针对他今天在会上提的问题，咱们还是找个解决方案吧。
Regarding the issues he raised today at the meeting, we had better work out a solution.

注意 (zhu yi): *pay attention* or something else

A careful linguist may be able to read something different from *pay attention to* in 注意.

It has two meanings:

➤ 注意 as *being attentive, keeping an eye on something*. In this case, 注意 is often followed by a noun. *Pay attention to* is the correct translation.

> 注意 as *making efforts to do something*. In this case, 注意 is often followed by a verb. One should use something else, depending on the context.

Examples:

> 我们要时刻注意价格的浮动情况
> We must pay attention to price fluctuations at all times.

> 我们要时刻注意掌握价格浮动的情况
> We must make efforts to get a grip on the price fluctuations at all times.

> 你要注意他脸上的表情
> You should pay attention to his facial expressions.

> 你要注意记录他的面部表情
> You should try to record his facial expressions.

> 人事部门要注意员工的反应
> The HR department should pay attention to employees' reactions.

> 人事部门要注意收集员工的反应
> The HR department should make an effort to collect employees' reactions.

> 家长要注意孩子们的学习情况
> Parents should pay attention to their children's school performance.

> ➢ 家长要注意改善孩子们的学习环境
> Parents should do their best to improve the learning environment for their children.

自动 (zi dong): *automatic* or *automated*

自动, in its adjective form, is often rendered as *automatic* and *automated*. It doesn't help much when one has to make a choice.

The difference between *automatic* and *automated* often spells the difference between good or poor translation.

Simply put, *automated* is about a process programmed to function in a desired way; thus, it is often used for describing processes, systems, production lines, mechanisms, and the like, ones that involve system operation.

Automatic, on the other hand, is about the effect of the above programmed processes; thus, it is often used for describing machines, equipment, tools, weapons, and so forth.

Automated is about mechanisms; *automatic* is about results.

Therefore, an *automated* weapon fires *automatically* once the trigger is pulled, because the firing mechanism is already *automated*. *Automatic* firing is the result of the *automated* firing system.

The firing is *automatic* because the triggering system is *automated*. When we talk about automatic weapons, we are talking about both its firing effect and its inner firing mechanism.

It is the same with an automatic teller machine (ATM). On the surface, your money comes out *automatically*, but for it to happen *automatically*, the mechanisms of identifying, counting, and dispensing must be programmed so that all three functions run in an *automated* manner, before you see money coming out *automatically*.

Next time, when you are faced with 自动, try to find out whether it is about system or effect, process or result.

Take 自动检测, for example. Is it *automatic* detection or *automated* detection? Without sufficient context, both *automatic* detection and *automated* detection would work.

But each is one side of the same coin. While *automatic detection* focuses on the alarm being set off when something is detected, *automated* detection is more about the steps programmed to set off the alarm.

One hears a "beep" when a metal detector detects a key chain. Let the key chain pass through the detector TEN times, and the detector would beep ten times. The <u>beep</u> is *automatic*.

What makes it beep is the automated mechanism, which is programmed to tell the detector to beep. From sensing a metal piece, to analyzing it, to triggering the alarm system, all steps are automated so that the detector beeps each time it detects a key chain.

Automatic detection is about the "beep"; *automated detection* is about the mechanism. In other words, the system is *automated*; the "beep" is *automatic*.

But watch out! When 自动 suggests 自愿 (willingness), 自觉 (conscious efforts), 主动 (voluntary), it is neither *automatic* nor *automated*.

Examples:

➢ 服务人员应自动介绍产品性能。
Sales representatives should take the initiative in explaining the product performance.

➢ 如遇紧急情况, 乘务人员应自动返回车组。
In emergency circumstances, crew members should return to the train on their own initiative.

> 你要自动把钱还给她。

You should give her back the money voluntarily.

> 你要自动向警方坦白交待。

You should confess everything to the police on your own accord.

> 他自动选择到一个边远的山区小学教书。

He volunteered to teach elementary school in a remote mountainous area.

> 耳朵发炎不必吃抗生素, 炎症自动会好。

No antibiotics are needed for ear infections, which can get better on their own.

总结 (zong jie): *summarize, review,* or *evaluate*

The term 总结 means two things: to sum up, to list things in a concise manner, more like 归纳, 汇总; and to review (evaluate) what went right and what went wrong, as guidance for future performance, more like 评价.

We often see 总结经验 translated as *summarize experience,* but again, this is a case of careless word-for-word translation.

What is 总结经验 trying to say? Answer: review past experience to find out what went right and what went wrong.

What is *summarize experience* trying to say? Answer: *present expertise in a concise manner.* It is 汇总经验.

Clearly, 总结经验 and *summarize experience* are talking past each other! A poor translation.

So 总结经验 means review, evaluate past performance so as to find what worked, what failed, and what best to do in the future. Therefore, the proper translation should be *evaluate the performance.*

In other words, 总结 is expressed in *review, evaluate past performance*, and 经验 is covered in *find what worked, what failed*, and *what best to do in the future*.

Context dictates whether 总结 means *list things in a concise manner* or *review, evaluate*.

Examples:

➤ 我把刚才说的总结一下
Let me sum up what I have just said.
(A gist, not an evaluation; no judgment is involved.)

➤ 本部门的年度工作总结报告详细列举了对过去一年工作的评估
The agency's Annual Performance Report presents a detailed assessment of the performance of last year.
(To say "summary report" is only to suggest an abridged version of what the agency did, but not what it did right and what failed. It fails to capture the meaning of 工作总结.)

➤ 今年的工作总结要在年底完成
This year's performance evaluation (review) must be completed by the end of the year.
(Again, it is an evaluation but a summary)

➤ 我们要认真总结一下过去两年我们所做的一切
We ought to make serious efforts to evaluate what we have done in the past two years.
(Assess what we did well and not so well in the past two years.)

> 救灾工作结束后，我们要总结一下，以利今后做得更好。
>
> After the relief operation is all over, we should evaluate our efforts so that we can do better moving forward.

> 在总结表彰大会上，我们团队获得"最佳顾客满意奖"。
>
> At the evaluation and recognition meeting, our team received the Best Customer Service Team award.

组织 (zu zhi): *organization* or something else

Translating 组织 to *organization* is completely harmless, until 组织 appears in its unique context, where it is no longer an ordinary organization.

The context has to do with the Chinese political culture. 组织, in this case, is synonymous to the Communist Party committees at all levels in all places. So,

> 有问题要及时向组织汇报 translates, *If you have any issues, you must report them to the Party Committee.*
> 有困难，找组织 translates, *If you need help, go to the Party Committee.*
> 你的休假计划要组织同意才行 translates, *Your plan to take a break must be approved by the Party Committee.*
> 要相信组织 translates. *We must have faith in the Party.*
> 组织要我干啥，就干啥 translates, *I will do whatever the Party wants me to do.*
> 在组织生活会上，要有什么说什么 translates, *At the Party Committee's heart-to-heart talk session, you should speak whatever is on your mind.*

Fortunately, when 组织 doesn't refer to the Communist Party or Party leadership, it can be translated safely to *organization*.

最后 (zui hou): *finally* or *lastly*

It is about 最后 used at the end of a list, as in 首先, …, 其次, …, 最后. But 最后 is often translated to *finally*.

It's wrong.

Finally suggests an end following long efforts, not a simple list of sequence. Its Chinese equivalent is 终于. With *finally*, the list would sound like this: First, …; second, …; at long last, …

Lastly is the correct translation of 最后 in this context.

做好 (zuo hao): *do well* or else

做好 has two meanings: (1) it is similar to 做得好 or 把 … 做好 (*do a good job of* …). The focus is on trying one's best; and (2), the word 好 serves as a suffix, attaching the meaning of "finish" to the verb. The focus is on finishing a task.

In the case of *do well*, we have:

➤ 政府号召有关部门帮助灾区做好灾后的重建工作。
The government calls on relevant agencies to do a good job in helping the disaster-hit areas with their reconstruction efforts.

➤ 做好今年的人口普查, 关键在不要放过边远地区的每家每户。
The key to a good census job for this year is visiting every household in remote areas.

In the case of *finish*, we have:

> 后勤部门要做好出发前的准备工作。

The logistics department should get things ready before we get started.

> 评委要在两个小时内做好考生资格复审工作。

Judges should complete the candidates' qualification reviews within two hours.

> 教委要求务必在八月做好问卷的审查工作。

The Education Commission requires that a review of questionnaire be completed in August.

Similar expressions with a 好 suffix also include:

> 吃好了, 就走吧, 别坐着了。

If you are done with your meal, you can leave now. Don't just sit there.

> 表填好了, 交给谁？

I have filled out the form. To whom should I give it?

> 推荐信写好了吗？

Have you finished your recommendation letter?

> 房子装修好了以后, 请你们过来坐坐。

After I am done with my house remodeling, I will invite you over.

> 晚上会见代表们的事我已经安排好了。

I have already made the arrangements for the meeting with the delegates in the evening.

作用 (zuo yong): *role, function, effect,* or *impact*

Here is a simple trick: 作用 often is paired up with different Chinese words to give us a telltale sign of one of the meanings above.

Therefore, 起 ··· 作用 and 在 ... 的作用 often take *role*; 有 ··· 作用 and 在 ··· 作用下 often take *function, effect, impact, action.*

Examples:

> 常用电脑的人时常望远, 能起到保健眼睛的作用。
>
> For those often working at the computer, looking in the distance every now and then can be effective in keeping their eyes healthy.

> 他在上一轮的谈判中起到了重要的作用
>
> He played an important role in the last round of negotiations.

> 你说的办法我试了, 一点作用都没有。
>
> I tried the method you suggested, but it didn't have any effect.

> 中成药在出厂十几年后, 成份有挥发作用。
>
> After a decade or so of shelf life, ready-to-use traditional Chinese medicines would see the effect of compromised efficacy of their ingredients.

"Honey, do we have to?"

Chapter 2

Punctuation—Where
East Meets West

> Good translation should be
> true to the original in spirit,
> in meaning, and in style.
>
> — Yan Fu (Chinese scholar
> and translator, 1854–1921)

In This Chapter

- ✓ Quotation Marks
- ✓ Punctuation around Quotation Marks
- ✓ Colon or Comma after 说
- ✓ Colon, the Chinese Way
- ✓ Punctuating Titles

In translation, punctuation marks do not seem to be a problem. They should not be. If the Chinese document has a comma, shouldn't the English version show a comma? Not quite so.

Did you know that the punctuation marks currently used in the Chinese language were originally not part of the Chinese language?

It was February 1868—yes, that long ago—when a group of Chinese scholars embarked on a long trip to Europe and the United States to learn about the West.

They found, much to their amazement, that the Westerners used a great variety of punctuation marks: " . " to indicate a stop, " ; " to suggest an additional sentence to the previous one, " ! " to express exclamation, " ? " to indicate a question, " " " " to show something being quoted, and so on and so forth.

This was eye-opening, among other discoveries—machines, railroads, locomotives, and so forth. Upon their return to China, they quickly drafted a motion to the emperor: we should adopt the Western punctuation marks.

Many scholars couldn't wait to try their hands at these newfound punctuation marks to add a touch of modernity to their writings. But they had to wait. It was not until fifty years later, in February 1920, that the Chinese government issued Decree No. 52 to start the official use of new punctuation marks, the ones we see today.

What did the Chinese do prior to this point when they needed to express a question, a pause, or an outcry? Well, since the Chinese wrote from right to left, and top down, they created their own punctuation marks, not many though: o, ↓, ^, ..., ____, and so forth, only for pause and emphasis. And they used them whichever way they found convenient—underneath, on top, to the right, to the left—and they came in all sizes, all to one's fancy.

However, most books were still without a single punctuation mark. How did the readers know when a sentence stopped and a new one began? Well, one had to be well schooled to master the trick.

Western punctuation marks currently used in China are like an adopted child of the Chinese language family, growing up in a Chinese linguistic environment, mixed with Chinese language logics.

Take the use of a comma ", " for example. The general rule for the use of a comma in the West is to introduce a pause, following certain rules. But when it is used in the Chinese language, often it is the case that after a long subject, the Chinese would pause; thus, a comma is used this way:

> 厂领导和各车间工人们, 冒着大雪清理通往工厂的车道
> The factory management and workers, braved the heavy snow and cleaned the road to the factory.

A funny thing is happening here. The Chinese language pauses the Chinese way, but it is expressed the Western way. This poses a problem when translation is involved, as is shown in the above translation, and the ones below:

1. Quotation Marks

Chinese and English languages share two traces of similarity, fortunately, in the use of quotation marks:

Direct quote:

> 他说他正在 "品尝" 自由。
> He said he was "tasting" freedom.

> 里根总统说: "好戏还在后头呢! "
> President Reagan said, "You ain't seen nothin' yet!"

Irony:

> "善良"的老板把员工一个一个都炒了鱿鱼。
> The "good-hearted" boss fired all of his employees.

> 他"理直气壮"地收受贿赂。
> He took bribes with a "clear conscience."

Well, there goes the easy part.
From this point on, the two languages part ways in the use of quotation marks and what they mean.

Where Chinese quotation marks express emphasis, the English translation might read irony.

> 本店出售"纯天然"饮用水
> Awkward translation: *We have "Pure Natural" drinking water.*
> (Is the water really pure and natural?)

> "大甩卖"! 买一送一 !
> Awkward translation: *"Free!" Buy One, Get One Free*
> (So, are they free after all?)

> 我们要做人民的"父母官"。
> Awkward translation: *We must be people's "benevolent officials."*
> (The so-called benevolent?)

> 他连续发了三个"电子邮件"。
> Awkward translation: *He sent three "e-mail messages" in a row.*
> (So, are those really e-mail messages or something else?)

➤ 可信计算技术的目的是要构建一个 "可信" 的计算环境。
   Awkward translation: *The objective of trusted computing techniques is to build a "trusted" computing environment.*
   (Is it trusted or not, after all?)

➤ 要保证所有的车辆 "开得动"。
   Awkward translation: *Make sure that all vehicles are "ready to go."*
   (Are they really ready when the moment comes?)

➤ 我们的政策是要让人们吃 "饱"。
   Awkward translation: *Our policy is to let people have "enough" to eat.*
   (Do you really want them to have enough?)

➤ 游泳前, 请 "冲澡"。
   Awkward translation: *Please "shower" before entering the pool.*
   (Is token sprinkling all right?)

➤ 我们是他的 "粉丝"。
   Awkward translation: *We are his "fans."*
   (Are you really his fans?)

Now you see where this is going. To avoid ambiguity, the English rendition can use italics, underline, or bold letters for emphasis in place of quotation marks.

Where Chinese quotation marks indicate proper nouns, English uses capitalization.

➤ 客人们今天参观了 "白宫" 和 "五角大楼"
   The guests visited the White House and the Pentagon today.

> "冷战" 期间, 美苏两国都在大规模地扩充军备.
> During the Cold War, the US and the USSR were both expanding their arms on a massive scale.

> 美国 "企业" 号航母已离开基地
> The USS *Enterprise* has already left the base.

> 比住帐篷稍贵一点的, 就是 "青年旅社".
> A little pricier than staying in a tent is staying in youth hostels.

Where Chinese quotation marks suggest special effect, English can do without.

For an unusual effect, the Chinese language often includes that particular special-effect phrase in quotation marks, be it a slang word, an idiom, a metaphor, or a description.

> 到国会去 "拉项目"
> Go to the Congress to solicit funds.
> ("拉项目" is often seen in business dealings; also, it's an informal way of saying, solicit a project.)

> 他们都说我在家里就像在 "象牙塔" 里
> They all say that staying at home, for me, is like being in an ivory tower.
> (A metaphor)

> 在饭桌旁, 县委书记和村民"唠家常"
> At the dinner table, the county Party secretary chatted with the villagers.

("唠家常" is often used to mean chitchat. Here, a county Party boss and farmers are not fit for "唠家常" in highly hierarchical China. Effect: the Party boss is showing humility.)

> 他从商店买来一个 "大家伙"
> He bought something very big from the store.
> ("家伙" is often used to refer to people. Effect: add a human touch to the merchandise.)

> 从马路对面走来一位"的哥"。
> There comes a taxi driver from across the street.
> ("的哥" is a newly coined term for taxi driver. Effect: a touch of endearment.)

> 他连续发了三个 "伊妹儿"。
> He sent three e-mail messages in a row.
> ("伊妹儿" is a transliteration of the word "e-mail," with a naughty twist.)

> 黄河是中华民族的 "摇篮"
> The Yellow River is the cradle of Chinese civilization.
> ("摇篮" is being used here as a metaphor.)

If the above quoted terms are rendered in English with quotation marks, they will read as if they were not what the writers intended them to mean.

A piece of advice for using colloquialisms from William Strunk Jr. and E. B. White:

"If you use a colloquialism or a slang word or phrase, simply use it; do not draw attention to it by enclosing it in quotation marks. To do so is to put on airs, as though you were inviting the reader to join you in a select society of those who know better."[4]

2. Punctuation around Quotation Marks

This is where one has to make major changes when translating Chinese documents. There is no uniform practice in the Chinese language in this regard; some punctuation is put outside the quotation marks and some inside, all depending on the writer's preference.

To ensure correct usage of punctuation in translation and to be consistent, one should follow the English rule.

One should also be aware of the different rules for American English and British English. In British English, logical quotation is the rule; namely, whether punctuation goes inside or outside depends on the logic of the sentence.

What is used here is the rule for American English.

Periods and commas go inside (with one exception: if the last word is a single letter or number, the period goes outside.)

> 那摞书上放着一个大大的 "X"。
> Above that pile of books place a huge "X".

> 他说: "办公室一个人都没有"。
> He said, "No one is in the office."

> 布告栏上写着: "今天下午的会取消了"。
> The bulletin reads, "This afternoon's meeting is canceled."

---

[4] William Strunk, Jr., and E. B. White, *The Elements of Style*, 4th ed. Longman, 1999.

➢ 人称她是"女包公"。
She is dubbed a "Lady *Bao Gong*."

➢ 门上清清楚楚地写着"闲人免进"。
The sign on the door clearly says "Authorized Personnel Only."

➢ 我们的政策是"开发国际市场"。
Our policy is, "Develop overseas markets."

Exclamation Point and Question Mark

The rule is simple. If the quoted expression is itself a question or exclamation, then the question or exclamation mark goes inside the closing quotation mark.

If it is the question or exclamation of the author, then the question or exclamation mark goes outside the closing quotation mark.

Examples:

Chinese Version	English Version
他问："为什么偏偏是我"？	He asked, "Why me?"
他是问"为什么偏偏是他"吗？	Did he ask "Why him"?
他大声喊着："抓贼呀"！	He shouted, "Stop the thief!"
大家快喊"抓贼"！	Quick, everybody shout "Stop the thief"!

Colons and Semicolons

They go outside the quotation marks.

Since almost all Chinese punctuation marks are placed outside question marks, there seems to be no problem with translation regarding colons and semicolons. The correct English usage should be as follows:

➢ The CEO told a gathering in his office of high officials, the "wise men": the crisis is far from over.

➢ The red dot on the little girl's forehead is a "footprint of God"; the whole village believed in it.

➢ There was another problem with the slogan "No More Layoffs": It suggested that the company had to find other ways to stay alive.

➢ He commented to the researchers briefing him on the "IT market and future": "If what you say is true, then we will have to look elsewhere for business."

There is no confusion in this regard. Both Chinese and English share the same rule.

3. Colon or Comma after 说

The Chinese word 说 is followed by a colon, as in 他说: "我不知道", consistent with the British English rule.

But in American English, "say" is followed by a comma, as in *He said, "I don't know."*

In other cases of colon, both Chinese and English follow a similar practice, as in the following examples:

Chinese Version	English Version
他指出: …	He points out: …
我要说的是: …	What I am saying is: …
其中包括: …	They include: …
我有一个主意: …	I have an idea: …

4. Colon, the Chinese Way

In the Chinese language, a colon is used to clarify the subject preceding the colon, much like in English:

✓ 有两种选择: 留下或离开
There are two choices: stay or leave.

"Stay or leave" clarifies the "two choices."

The Chinese stretches a colon a little further, not as a clarification but as a regular comma.

Let's take a look at the following math equation:

➤ $N = (C + 100)$
式中: N为出席人数

Awkward translation: In the equation: N represents the number of people present.

Logic of a colon says that "N represents the number of people present" is the equation, much like the example above: "stay or leave" are the two choices.

But "N represents the number of people present" is not the equation. $N = (C + 100)$ is the equation. N is just one item.

What causes the confusion? The colon in "式中:".

Of course, the reader would quickly make a mental correction to make it read,

  ✓ *In the equation, N represents the number of people present.* Or,
  ✓ *Where N represents the number of people present.*

What is the linguist's job in this case? Keep the colon, and let readers make the correction? Or correct it to reflect where such an expression is normally written?

Clearly, drop the colon in translation to avoid confusion.

Such is translation, in the true sense of the word!

Let's take a look at another example:

➤ 照片中: 我当时只有十八岁。

In the picture, I am only eighteen years old.

But when translated with a colon, as

➤ *In the picture: I am only eighteen years old*

It might read that "I am only eighteen years old" is the name of the picture. Though a bit of a stretch here, the slight awkwardness can hurt the flow in reading nonetheless. After all, we don't say, "In the office: we can sit twenty people," or "In the US: there are many national parks."

5. Punctuating Titles

The Chinese language uses « » as the marks for books, magazines, and long documents, as in «美国宪法» (The United States Constitution) or «时代周刊» (*Time*).

The English translation, however, should follow the English language rules, regardless of what Chinese documents use.

Use italics as follows:

- ✓ *The Elements of Style*
- ✓ *Time* magazine
- ✓ *Reader's Digest*

Use quotation marks for titles of short works, such as articles, songs, short stories, and the like:

- ✓ "Fortune Cookies" in *Reader's Digest*
- ✓ "Punctuation" in *Handbook for Writers*
- ✓ "Smell of Spring" in *Collected Poems*

Chapter 3

What Makes a Good Translation After All?

> Translation should fully represent the ideas, the style of the original and should possess the ease of the original composition.
>
> --Alexander Fraser Tytler (Scottish writer and historian, 1747–1813)

In This Chapter

- ✓ End User-Oriented Translation
- ✓ Message-Oriented Translation
- ✓ Style-Oriented Translation

Well, the criterion is set by Mr. Tytler, clear and simple. All one needs to do is follow them.

Easily said. A lot goes into a good translation: knowledge of the cultures of the two languages involved, the style of the writer, standards set by the reader, and so forth, not to mention structural requirements to add or delete elements to meet the target language rules.

Good translation, as it turns out, is a delicate balancing act. It is never a clear-cut choice of right over wrong.

In some cases, good translation is in the eyes of the beholder. And the beholder is often the end user, not the good-translation theories.

Below is just a glimpse of the daunting task facing every linguist in real-life translation: to follow the great teachings or to follow what the circumstances demand you to do.

1. End User-Oriented Translation

Here is the rule: the linguist should follow the rules of the target language.

In other words, when translating Chinese into English, the linguist should follow the rules that govern the English language, namely how to express tenses, how to use punctuations, how to structure a sentence, how to make noun and verb agree, where to place footnote numbers, and so forth.

With this principle, producing a good translation should not be a problem, until your customer demands otherwise.

The official English translation of 五年计划 is *Five-Year Plan*. It is used in Chinese official English language media, such as *China Daily, Xinhua News, The New York Times*, and the like.

The rule is set. All one needs to do is follow it. Simple, or so it seems.

But, in one instance, one of my clients demanded that 五年计划 be translated as *Five-Year Program*.

What would you do? Protest? Cite the Chinese government's English version as a proof?

You can do all the kicking and screaming. But, eventually, the end user would simply tell you: either you translate it as *Five-Year Program*, or you lose your contract.

In another instance, where a superscript footnote marker/number placement is involved, one of clients insisted that the English version follow the Chinese style— footnote number precedes the punctuation, instead of the common English style— footnote number follows the punctuation, as shown below:

> ➢ Chinese style: 他终于买下了那座世纪豪宅 [1] 。
> ➢ Client's style: *He finally bought that Century Mansion* [1].
> ➢ Common English style: *He finally bought that Century Mansion.* [1]

In these two instances (there are millions more such cases), rules governing the usage of English language are overruled by the end user's rules. The linguist ends up with a painful choice: you either lose your job, or bend your principle.

What happens to good translation?

Well, in customer service, you want to make your customers happy. They are happy when they like the translation; they like your translation, because it is good in their eyes.

2. Message-Oriented Translation

One night, I was watching a World War II movie on TV. A group of US Marines were entering a concentration camp in Poland. As they pushed open the gate, they saw Jewish prisoners lying on the ground. Many were too weak to stand. Some were dying.

To catch the German soldiers, a US Marine, who could speak Polish, asked one Jewish prisoner where the German soldiers were. The frightened prisoner mustered what little strength he had left and said a few words. The marine quickly told his captain, "The Germans left two days ago."

Six words. Less than two seconds. But it took the prisoner forever to say these words.

Did the marine give a good translation? He did, in terms of getting the information across; he did not, in terms of mirroring the way the frightened Jewish prisoner said those words.

Often, an intelligence officer in the heat of a battle, a politician on a campaign trail, or a CEO keen on the company's performance are only interested in the message and only the message, not in how it is expressed.

A classic example of "message-oriented translation" is in translating for King George VI, the stuttering British king. Consider this scene: King George VI is delivering a speech to, say, a group of Chinese guests. His speech is then translated without a single stutter whatsoever.

Clearly, all that is needed is his message, not how he says it.

Such is "message-oriented translation"—and a good one–but it deviates a bit from Alexander Fraser Tytler's theory: *mirror both message and style.*

One day as I was driving home from work, NPR news announced the following over the radio: the 2006 Nobel Peace Prize was awarded jointly to Muhammad Yunus and the Grameen Bank in Bangladesh for their efforts in creating economic and social opportunities.

How do you translate "create economic and social opportunities"? 创造经济与社会机会? The Chinese may say 创造机会 (*create opportunities*) all right, but do they say 经济机会 (*economic opportunities*), 社会机会 (*social opportunities*)? I doubt it.

I know what the Chinese phrase 经济与社会机会 is trying to say. According to common usage, 机会 is the second part of an activity, often expressed with a verb; namely, the opportunity to do something, such as

➤ 就业机会 (job opportunities: to work);
➤ 发展机会 (development opportunities: to develop);

> ➤ 投资机会 (investment opportunities: to invest);
> ➤ 合作机会 (collaboration opportunity: to collaborate);
> ➤ 学习机会 (learning opportunity: to learn), and so forth.

But 经济与社会机会 (*economic and social opportunities*) are *not* used in this pattern, thus failing to suggest *an opportunity to do things.*

I know what the English phrase *economic and social opportunities* is trying to say: *to create opportunities for people to improve their economic conditions and social status.* Yes, this much is implied.

So the translation for *economic and social opportunities* should be 创造改善经济与社会地位的机会. By adding the terms 改善 and 地位, it is now clear, without compromising its original meaning.

A good translation.

3. Style-Oriented Translation

"朕要出恭" and "我要上茅房" say the same thing: *I want to use the bathroom.*

But to translate the first one, not only should the linguist get the message across, but he or she should also make sure an aristocratic tone is reflected. This was how the Chinese emperors said it when nature called.

Similarly, translation for the second bathroom expression should also cover both message and style, just so readers are clear that a farmer, not an emperor, is saying it.

Reversing them would produce a comic result, to say the least.

Likewise, Abraham Lincoln's Gettysburg Address should be translated to read as simple and elegant, not big-worded and aristocratic. *Tea House* (茶馆) by Chinese writer Lao She (老舍) should be translated to reflect his use of everyday words. Deng

Xiaoping's "cat theory"; namely, "不管黑猫白猫, 能抓老鼠的, 就是好猫" should be translated in such a way that his no-nonsense, matter-of-fact style gets across faithfully.

Some translations make his cat theory read too flowery to reflect any trace of Deng. For example, "A black plum is as sweet as a white one," or "All are fish that come to the net." The message may be Deng's, but the style is someone else's, for sure.

Years ago, I was interpreting for a panel of lawyers from a US government agency who were questioning the CEO of a Chinese firm. When pressed whether he was at a particular meeting, here is how the CEO tried to answer:

> "我想说 ..., 嗯 ..., 当时, 怎么说呢 ..., 那个 ... 其实 ... 我是说 ..., 反正 ..., 我 ..., 是这样 ..., 没 ... 那什么 ... 参加 ... 那个会."

At long last, he was finished.

After putting together all the bits and pieces of usable information, my interpretation went:

> *I was not at the meeting at the moment.*

The government lawyers got what they wanted and moved on to the next set of questions. To them, my interpretation served the purpose and was good.

But had this been a psychiatric evaluation session, the evaluators would have wanted to hear everything: every stutter, every repetition, every hesitation, every pause, every *um*, every *you know*, every *I mean*. Each of these seemingly meaningless utterances would carry a significant load of information to reveal the mental state of the speaker at the moment.

If I filtered out these elements and gave them only the processed information—*I was not at the meeting at the moment*—I would be killing the very purpose of the interview: psychiatric evaluation. Thus, my interpretation would have been bad, very bad.

Similarly, to translate King George VI's speech for a speech therapist, one must faithfully render every stutter so that not only what the king is trying to say is presented but how he is saying it—or, more importantly, how bad his stutter is—so that the therapist can assess the king's situation and come up with the appropriate treatment.

What happens, then, to that ultimate goal: faithful translation?

Well, it is relative, after all. It all depends on which criterion one uses to judge. A linguist must be capable of quickly finding the criterion for that situation.

Good translation is in the eye of the beholder, indeed.

Who says translation is not art!

"It's Mr. Wang, inviting us to dinner. How many times am I supposed to say 'no' to mean 'yes'?"

Chapter 4

Implied, Implied, Implied

> **Good translation is achieved through either semantic or communicative methods, with the former focusing on the what the message is trying to say as a whole, and the latter on which part of the message is useful to the audience.**
>
> **— Peter Newmark (British professor of translation, 1916–2011)**

In This Chapter

✓ **Ten Awkward Translations**

You must have had this experience: you have a Chinese sentence in front of you. You read it and get the message, or so it seems. You start to translate.

But your translation sounds awkward. It doesn't seem to get the message across, either in logic or in common sense. Some words are apparently missing in the Chinese sentence, words that are necessary to make your translation meaningful.

Well, welcome to the victims camp of "implied words"! Chinese sentences are never short of such "implied words."

Implied—and therefore missing—words are never a problem to native Chinese eyes (or ears). This ability to understand the implied message is in the DNA of native Chinese speakers, born and educated in the culture of implied messages. They can pick their way through the maze of implications and read between the lines. But for non-native Chinese linguists, it is a daunting challenge.

How do you get the message across, in translation, when a key word is not present? Well, the linguist must put the missing words back in the translation. Otherwise, awkward translation would result.

Here are some typical cases of necessary words being implied. The take-away of these cases is, I hope, to alert linguists to this linguistic landmine.

Ten Awkward Translations

Case No. 1

➢ 在事故恢复期间，各部门留人坚守岗位。

Awkward translation: *All departments should have someone on duty during the malfunction restoration period.*

What does *malfunction restoration* mean? Don't we fix malfunctions? Don't we recover from malfunctions? Don't we avoid malfunctions at all costs?

Implied, implied, implied. What is being implied is the part in the parenthesis: 在事故 (处理以便*be fixed so as to*) 恢复生产期间. So, it is actually trying to say, *All departments should have someone on duty during the period when we are trying to fix the malfunction and resume operation.*

When two concepts—*malfunction* and *resume operation*—are put together, common sense and logic dictate that it has to be understood as *fix the malfunction so that operation may resume.*

How does one know what is being implied? In this case, the translated version—*malfunction restoration* (or *restore malfunction*)—should raise a red flag immediately. It should not be a problem for a careful linguist.

Reading through the translation is often an effective way of finding whether an implied meaning is lost. If the translation sounds awkward, chances are something is being implied. The linguist is translating just the words, not the meaning.

Speaking of translating the meaning, not just words, here is a classic case:

We translate 不客气, in response to 谢谢, as "You are welcome," translating the meaning, not "Don't be polite" (translating the words). It's a beautiful translation!

But I digress.

Case No. 2

> 腹腔注射120 mg/kg 庆大霉素, 连续十天。
> **Awkward translation**: *IP injection of 120 mg/kg gentamicin for ten days in a row*

The dosage administered is not clear in the translation. How is the 120 mg/kg administered? Evenly spread out over ten days, 12 mg/kg a day? Or how many times a day? Or 120 mg/kg once a day for ten days? Common sense, in this particular matter, dictates that it has to be the last choice: *once a day for ten days.*

The Chinese version is clear because the implied part—120 mg/kg per day—is taken into account. It is almost always the case; a dosage is administered a certain number of times a day for a certain number of days (or months).

For the same result, the translation has to spell out the implied "per day" part, unless the above English version without "per day" renders the same unmistakably clear message.

A better translation should be: *IP injection of 120 mg/kg gentamicin a day, ten days in a row.* After all, isn't that a common instruction on a doctor's note—how much a day for how many days?

Case No. 3

> 天然植物可在一定程度上改善微波辐射对神经细胞的
> 损伤作用。
> **Awkward translation**: *To a certain degree, natural plants can improve microwave radiation's neural cells damage role.*

What does 天然植物改善 … 损伤作用 (*natural plants improve the damage role*) mean? It is ambiguous, to say the least. We reverse damage; we don't improve damage, unless we mean to cause more damage. Isn't *improve the damage role* trying to say it would cause more damage? Obviously, it is not the case.

What makes the translation awkward is the implied part. Thus, a key message is lost. According to Chinese logic, it actually reads:

> 天然植物可在一定程度上, (有) 改善微波辐射对神经细胞损
> 伤 (状况) 的作用
> *To a certain degree, natural plants can play a role in reducing damage to neural cells by microwave radiation.*

The part of 有 … 状况的作用 (*play a role in … condition*) is implied.

Case No. 4

> 二次大战期间, 英国工业基础雄厚, 支持战争潜力大。
> **Awkward translation**: *During WWII, the UK had a strong industrial foundation and a great potential to support the war.*

Support the war? It is ambiguous.

The context clearly suggests that *war* does not simply mean WWII (no rational person would support that war or any war) but the UK's war effort; thus, *the UK had a great potential to support her war effort.*

The Chinese version nevertheless makes sense on the same contextual understanding; therefore, it boldly implies that 支持战争 (*support the war*) actually means 支持打这一场战争 (*support the effort to fight the war*).

Again, common sense logic dictates how the sentence is to be read or how not to lose the implied part.

Case No. 5

> 由于节假日客流增长较大, 时间集中, 铁路部门要做好安排。
> **Awkward translation**: *During holidays, passenger flow would increase significantly and time would be concentrated, railway authorities should make proper arrangement.*

What does *time would be concentrated* mean?

Well, to native Chinese readers, the Chinese wording is clear: *people travel in the same time frame.*

But why does the translation read so awkwardly, with *time would be concentrated*? The implied part is missing; namely, *people's travel time is concentrated in the same time frame.*

To bring out the implied part, the Chinese version should read like this:

> 由于节假日客流增长较大，(客流) 时间集中，铁路部门要做好安排

Clear translation: *During holidays, passenger flow would increase significantly and concentrate in the same time frame. Railway authorities should make proper arrangements.*

So, you see, *passenger flow* is assumed. It is the passengers, not the time, who flock to train stations in the same time frame.

Case No. 6

> 不符合这些技术条件要求的装载方案, 都属于不合理装载。
> **Awkward translation**: *Any loading plan that does not comply with the technical requirements would be considered improper loading.*

A loading plan is considered improper loading? The collocation is not right. A plan can be a good plan or a poor plan. How can a *plan* be *loading*?

A native Chinese would read it with the implied meaning assumed: … *would be considered an improper loading plan.*

Aha! The word *plan* is implied in *an improper loading plan.*

Solution: put the word *plan* back in the translation, just so the translation makes sense—the same sense as the Chinese version.

Clear translation: *Any loading plan that does not comply with the technical requirements would be considered an improper loading **plan**.*

Case No. 7

> 对于不同的模型, 具有不同的操作方法和性能。
> **Awkward translation**: *For different models have different operation methods and performance.*

What is being implied? The subject, *models*. The two words 对于 throw the sentence off balance, from a translation point of view.

The full Chinese sentence should be:

> 不同的模型具有不同的操作方法和性能 (dropping the first two words 对于); or

> 对于不同的模型来说， 它们具有不同的操作方法和性能 (adding 来说 to complete the 对于 … 来说 structure, and adding a subject 它们 for the main clause).

Clear translation (with the implied portion translated):
As far as different models are concerned, they have different operation methods and performance.

Case No. 8

> 如图6所示为性能曲线
> **Awkward translation**: *As Figure 6 shows performance curves.*

This is a common expression for diagrams and figures in science and technology documents.

What is being implied? The subject, again.

The full Chinese sentence should be:

> 如图6所示, 曲线为性能曲线 (*As shown in Figure 6, the curves are the performance curves.*); or
> 图6所示为性能曲线 (*What Figure 6 shows are the performance curves.*); or
> 图6所示性能曲线 (*Figure 6 shows the performance curves.*).

Case No. 9

> 调查表明, 影响判断误差的因素主要包括: 理解误差和
沟通误差。
>
> **Awkward translation**: *Survey shows, factors affecting judgment errors include mainly: understanding error and communication error.*

What does *factors affecting judgment errors* mean? How do they affect judgment errors? How do they affect errors? Don't factors affect judgment?

Something is apparently not right. And something is apparently missing or implied.

Logic dictates that the full Chinese sentence should be: 调查表明, 影响判断**而导致**误差的因素主要包括: 理解误炸和沟通误差 (Survey shows, factors affecting judgment *and causing* errors include mainly understanding errors and communication errors.)

So 而导致 (*so as to cause*) is implied. When the Chinese eyes sweep across the sentence, the implied part doesn't seem to be a problem, but Western eyes are not wired this way.

Case No. 10

> 我爱地球上每个生命, 唯独对蟑螂无法克服!
>
> **Awkward translation**: *I love every life on earth, but I just can't overcome cockroaches!*

This is a remark by 阿雅 (Aya Liu), an actress and talk-show host. I found this on her qq.com website. Pretty cute. But what does she mean by *overcome cockroaches*? Don't we overcome difficulties, loneliness, fear, and the like?

Apparently, she doesn't mean *kill cockroaches*. Not at all. She loves life—all lives.

What exactly does she mean by *overcome?*

Well, implied, implied, implied. What is being implied is what comes after 克服 (*overcome*). In fact, she is trying to say, *overcome the fear (or disgust) of cockroaches.*

So, the full Chinese sentence should be:

> 我爱地球上每个生命, 唯独对蟑螂无法克服恐惧感!
>
> I love every life on earth, but I just can't overcome *the fear of* cockroaches!

The ten cases are just a dip into the vast ocean of implied messages, a Chinese phenomenon.

They may be occasional occurances, but are enough to raise a red flag, warning linguists, "Hey, if your translation reads awkwardly, perhaps you should check whether some Chinese words are implied."

A quick cure: use logic and common sense.

if your translation doesn't sound logical, as in Aya's cockroaches comment (Case No. 10)—that she would kill cockroaches after claiming she loves every life on earth—you must be in the "implied" wonderland.

If your translation goes against common sense, as in Case No. 9—factors affecting judgment errors—then maybe you should see where the key words are missing.

How can Chinese so blatantly imply, without fearing being misunderstood?

I can only guess it is the culture.

The closest analogy to the effortless capture of the implied message among Chinese is a group of friends in a restaurant, fighting to pay for the meal. All know full well who will eventually pay, but they fight in all earnestness nonetheless.

Mr. Payer is implied long before the fight.

Such is the art of translation.

"Oh, no. I am more incapable than you are."

Chapter 5

To Translate or Not to Translate

> 译成之文能使阅者所得之
> 意，与观原文无异．
>
> **The translated version should
> benefit the readers in such a way
> as if they were reading the original.**
>
> **-- 马建忠 Ma Jianzhong
> (Chinese scholar, 1844–1900)**

In This Chapter

- ✓ **Extra Words**
- ✓ **Four-Word Phrases**
- ✓ **Summary Ending**
- ✓ **Street Address**
- ✓ **Personal and Place Names**

Well, this chapter is more about what *not* to translate. It is always easy—and tempting—to translate everything, but it is much harder not to translate, with the words right in front of you.

Again, who says translation is not art!

The two languages, Chinese and English, operate in two systems, each with its own rules—some mutually shared; most amazingly different.

When the rules are the same, the linguist has an easy time. 我要面条 automatically translates: *I want noodles.* Subject-verb-object; everything is in the matching order. It's the dream result for a linguist!

But when the two rules are talking past each other, the linguist will be in for a hard time.

Some of the rules are so Chinese that no English equivalent can be found, such as those ever-present four-word phrases, figurative expressions, and many more. In most cases, mirror imaging these styles in English translation only confuses the readers.

Often in translation, linguists find themselves torn between the two rules: if they follow the Chinese rules, their translation would have every element rendered (they'd be comforted that they have everything covered), but it would sound awkward. If they follow the English rules, their translation would have to omit some Chinese elements (they're guilty of not translating everything), but it would flow smoothly.

It is comforting to know that when the two rules meet, the target language (译文)—English, in this case—prevails over the source language (原文)—Chinese, in this case.

With that principle in mind, the linguist should know what to translate and what not to translate, all for the purpose of smooth reading, without compromising the message.

Below are some typical cases where linguists have to make that decision.

Extra Words

Extra words are often added to a sentence, written and spoken, for cosmetic purposes, but when translated into English, the same extra words appear as a redundancy, seriously compromising the meaning.

   ✓ **Rule of thumb:** Don't translate the extra words if you can still get the exact message across.

Example 1:

➢ 医疗水平的高低, 教学质量的好坏, 施工范围的大小, 服务态度的优劣。
  Awkward translation: *The high or low level of medical service, the good or bad quality of education, the big or small of the scope of construction, and the good or bad of the attitude.*

The last two words (高低, 好坏, 大小, 优劣) of the above phrases are classic structural touch-ups. They help put rhythm to the Chinese phrases, but they don't add anything to the meaning. Their role is simply to make the phrases read at a set beat.

In terms of meaning, they are useless. 水平 (*level*) covers the meaning of 高低 (*high or low*); 质量 (*quality*) covers the meaning of 好坏 (*good or bad*); 范围 (*scope*) covers the meaning of 大小 (*big or small*); 态度 (*attitude*) encompasses the meaning of 优劣 (*good or bad*).

Now, you get the picture.

Not translating those words apparently doesn't hurt the translation in structure and, more importantly, in meaning.

Example 2:

> 今年的销售统计报告资料已准备完毕
> **Awkward translation**: *This year's sales statistics report data is ready.*

This is another structural touch-up case, all for the sake of having four words in each of the two sense groups: 销售统计 (*sales statistics*) and 报告资料 (*report data*). Symmetrical for Chinese structure but frustrating for English translation.

In this case, the two words—资料 (*data*) immediately following 报告 (*report*)—are for cosmetic purposes only. They make the Chinese phrases balanced, but they don't add anything meaningful to the message. If translated, they would mess up the intended message.

Report data? Isn't *data* what is in the report? Doesn't the *report* contain *data*? The content of the *report* is *data*, after all.

Well, let me play devil's advocate here. What if the word *data* has its own meaning? What if, by *sales statistics report data,* the word *data* means the data necessary for preparing the sales statistics report?

It may very well be the case, but the Chinese wording would have been, most likely, 今年的销售统计报告用的资料已准备完毕, with the two words 用的 before *data* to mean "data needed for the report." The translation would have been "The data *needed for* this year's sales statistics report is ready."

Of course, not all Chinese sentences are written in a word-savvy manner. If 今年的销售统计报告资料已准备完毕 (without the two critical words 用的) does mean "The data *needed for* this year's sales statistics report is ready," then the linguist will be left with two choices: the *report* is ready, or the *data* is ready.

It is a challenging job. A careful linguist should look into the context to make the final call.

Translation, after all, is never a black-and-white mathematical science. It is an art. As such, a lot depends on how you understand the sentence in its context.

But often, unfortunately, even the context is not clear. That makes translation all the more, say, frustrating.

Example 3:

> 把党章权威竖起来, 立起来
>
> **Awkward translation**: *The authority of the Party's Constitution must be established and installed.*

Aren't 竖起来 (*establish*), 立起来 (*establish*) saying the same thing? In the Chinese lexicon, 竖 and 立, together, is a verb phrase, meaning *establish*. By separating the verb, the author is playing a word game only possible in Chinese.

It is for the effect of emphasis.

The closest equivalent, if any, in English may be *established* and *recognized*. This is the best—or worst—I can do to draw an analogy. It may match the Chinese two-word format, but it is being redundant nonetheless. To establish an authority *is* for it to be recognized.

To drive home the point, the awkward translation sounds as awkward as if one were to say, "The house must be built and constructed."

Solution: *The authority of the Party's Constitution must be established.* Take off one *establish,* and one can still get the message across perfectly.

Example 4:

> 发展畜牧业生产基地
>
> **Awkward translation**: *Develop animal husbandry production base.*

The message is not clear.

Is it talking about raising animals or producing animal products? Animal husbandry does two things: it raises livestock for breeding purposes, and it produces milk, beef cattle, and wool, among other commercial goods.

So 生产基地 (*production base*) only gives part of the picture. 畜牧业, as an industry, indicated by the suffix 业, has the meaning 生产 (*production*) covered. In fact, in many official Chinese documents, 畜牧业基地 is used instead, without adding 生产.

But why do we see 生产基地 in this case? It again has to do with Chinese political culture.

In Chinese political ideology, 生产 (*produce*) is synonymous with what the working class does, as opposed to 剥削 (*exploit*), what the bourgeoisie does, a bad concept in Chinese political ideology.

Thus, 生产 has an inherent political correctness. A good thing. A word with a good meaning. Add 生产 to a business activity, and it will become a noble cause.

So, a 畜牧业生产基地 is no more or less than a 畜牧业基地, as Chinese official documents call it. Simply, *animal husbandry base.*

Take off 生产, and you still keep the meaning intact and smooth the sentence flow.

Example 5:

> 他先后七次修改讲稿
>
> **Awkward translation**: *He revised his manuscript seven times one after another.*

Linguists are sometimes tempted to translate 先后 to *one after another*, urged by the obligation to render faithful translations, often understood as "no word left behind." But translating 先后 can do more harm than good.

I can see readers scratch their heads when they read, "He revised his manuscript seven times one after another."

Logic dictates that the "seven times" can never happen all at once. They have to be happening at different times, by logic and by common sense. The two words 先后 are simply trying to say "from the earliest (先) revision to the last (后) one," suggesting a time span.

It is perfectly all right to take off 先后 in translation, without compromising the message. Not a bit. The translation now reads like an English sentence: *He revised his manuscript seven times.*

Example 6:

> 当角度大于0.3⁰以上时, 运行趋于稳定。
>
> **Awkward translation**: *When the angle is greater than 0.3⁰ and above, operation becomes stable.*

This is about a technical issue, a classic case of mixing the spoken style with the written one.

Nothing wrong with the spoken style, but when the two are mixed, inconsistency results.

Spoken Chinese (or any language) tends to be loosely structured and repetitive. As long as people get the message, the utterance quickly goes out the other ear.

当角度大于0.3⁰时 (*When the angle is greater than 0.3⁰*) is perfectly clear. But somehow, the author throws in 以上 (*above*), as he would do when talking, assuming that any degree greater than *0.3⁰* is above *0.3⁰*. Hence, the spoken style: 当角度大于0.3⁰以上时 (*When the angle is greater than 0.3⁰ and above*).

Greater than 0.3⁰ and above? It doesn't make sense. If it is greater than *0.3⁰*, isn't it already greater than degrees above *0.3⁰*? Isn't any degree greater than 0.3 above 0.3?

You can see when logic dictates that the extra 以上 is unnecessary, don't translate it.

Four-Word Phrases

There are two types of four-word phrases: idioms and slang, and improvised four-word phrases.

There are tons of literature and translations of idioms. They are not what I am after; I am interested in the second type. And these are the ones that cause awkward translations.

Four-word phrases often appear in parallel structure, a set of two, sometimes three or more. If they follow the same format, they make beautiful parallels, and the linguist would have an easy time translating them.

Often, that is not the case. When the author groups four words simply for the sake of making the structure symmetrical, the linguist would have to be on high alert. Just because the first four-word phrase is logical and makes sense doesn't mean the next one is.

✓ **Rule of thumb:** If they are idioms, find a dictionary or go online to find established translations. If they are grouped by the author, meaning takes priority over structure.

Example 1:

➢ 本文主要涉及数据通讯与指挥控制
Clumsy translation: *This paper is mainly about data communication and command control.*

数据通讯与指挥控制 (*data communication and command control*) has two sets of four-word phrases, one on each side, separated by 与 (*and*) and symmetrically structured.

However, when translated into English, the symmetry becomes a problem. While the first four words—数据通讯 (*data communication*)—is a one-sense unit, saying one thing, expressing one idea, the other four words—指挥控制 (*command control*)—is not. It is a two-sense unit, saying two things, expressing two ideas: command and control.

A lethal temptation is to translate it to *data communication and command control* to match the Chinese format. At least the English version looks as balanced as its Chinese format: two words, if not four, on each side of "*and*." Perfect match!

But it is wrong. 指挥控制 is not *command control*—someone controls the command? Or someone commands the control?

The linguist must part with the symmetry format and save the message at all costs. The correct translation should be "data communication, command, and control."

There goes the structural symmetry.

Example 2:

> 多年的GPS 应用实践证明, 它是目前最有效的导航工具.
> **Clumsy translation**: *Years of application practice proves that GPS is currently the most effective guidance tool.*

应用实践 (*application practice*) is an improvised four-word phrase. But two of the four words are unnecessary. Application is itself a practice of using GPS, isn't it? The idea of 实践 (*practice*) is already expressed in 应用 (*application*).

Why bother adding it?

Well, long story short. It all has to do with China's culture of political correctness. Somehow, the word 实践 (*practice*) has an inherent political correctness, partly because of Chairman Mao's work *On Practice* (实践论) and Deng Xiaoping's theory of *practice* is the sole benchmark for testing truth (实践是检验真理的唯一标准) and countless statements containing the words 实践, such as 实践证明 … (*practice proves* …), statements that are often followed by what turns out to be correct.

The term 实践 (*practice*) has taken on a magic power of its own: 实践 (*practice*) = politically correct. Thus, an activity coupled with the word 实践 is often an indication that it is now being done for a politically correct reason.

Anything that is part of 实践 (*practice*) would automatically be a good cause. Therefore, consciously or subconsciously, people like to add 实践 to the activities in which they are engaged.

For correct translation, don't translate 实践.

Example 3:

> 广大职工在铁路生产实践活动中，充分利用高科技，创造了更高的经济效益。
>
> **Clumsy translation:** *In the railway operation practice activities, staff made the most of high technologies and achieved a higher level of productivity.*

Here is an even more blatant case of unnecessary words being piled up on an already clear message, all for the sake of forming a four-word phrase: 铁路生产实践活动 (*railway production practice activities*).

Railway production practice activity seems to be saying a lot but in fact says very little. Isn't *railway production* a practice and thus an activity, in and of itself? Why add *practice* and *activity*? Aren't the meanings already present in *production*?

Well, the phrase sounds better with two parallels, each with a four-word phrase: 铁路生产 and 实践活动. But when translated into a foreign language, meant for foreign readers, with *practice* and *activity* translated, the clumsiness kills the message.

The correct translation should be, "In railway production, staff made the most of high technologies and achieved a higher level of productivity."

Example 4:

> 春运时期的车辆调度，要根据天气情况，运力条件，时限要求，客流大小等情况而定。
>
> **Clumsy translation:** *During the Spring Festival traffic peak season, trains should be dispatched based on weather condition, transport capacity condition, deadline requirement, and passenger flow volume, among other conditions.*

This is a different case. In some four-word phrases, all four words can be translated, while in others, the four words have to be cut short. And it is all happening in one sentence.

Simple rule: translate or not; it is all dictated by how the English expression goes. Let's dissect each of the four-word phrases above.

We say *weather conditions* when talking about weather. So all four words of 天气情况(*weather condition*) can be translated. Translation: *weather conditions*.

We say *transport capacity* when talking about how many passengers a train can take. So only the first two words of 运力条件 (*transport capacity condition*) need to be translated, assuming *capacity* is itself a 条件 (*condition*). Translation: *transport capacity*.

We say *deadline* when talking about meeting a given point in time as a requirement. So only the first two words of 时限要求 (*deadline requirement*) need to be translated. Translation: *deadline*.

We say *passenger flow* (or *traffic volume*) when talking about how many passengers take the train at a given time. So only the first two words of 客流大小 (*passenger flow volume*) need to be translated. Translation: *passenger flow*.

More such cases where the last two words can be ignored:

➤ 职位高低 (rank)
➤ 资历深浅 (seniority)
➤ 成就大小 (accomplishment)
➤ 收入多少 (income)
➤ 速度快慢 (speed)
➤ 气温高低 (temperature)
➤ 个头高矮 (height)
➤ 尺寸大小 (size)
➤ 价格高低 (price)
➤ 质量好坏 (quality)

> 水位深浅 (water level)
> 态度好坏 (attitude)

The list can go on and on.

The last two words are only there to add a beat. The linguist can safely ignore them in translation.

Example 5:

> 有些人热衷于打探消息, 四处询问, 八方打听。
>
> **Clumsy translation**: *Some people are interested in inquiring about others, asking around and inquiring around.*

This is a classic case of piling up four-word phrases not for meaning but for structural balance.

In this case, the linguist's job is to make sure the part of the sentence containing the core meaning is translated. The piled-up parts for structural balance should be rendered to flow with the English structure rules.

In the sentence above, the message gets across perfectly all right in 有些人热衷于打探消息 (*Some people are interested in inquiring about others*). The following piled-up parts 四处询问 (*inquiring about others all around*) and 八方打听 (*asking around about others*) are wordplay, with 四处 (in four places) echoing 八方 (in eight directions), and 询问 (*inquiring about*) echoing 打听 (*asking around*).

Now, how on earth can the linguist match Chinese wordplay with English phrases?

Very hard. To follow the principle of translating both meaning and genre as best as one can, one can translate the wordplay part where English structure rules allow. In this case, the best possible translation is, "Some people are interested in inquiring about others, always nosing around."

Example 6:

> 对信息流程的日常管理和监督维护
> **Clumsy translation**: *Routine management and supervision maintenance of information flow.*

The English version matches the Chinese four-word phrases—one on each side of 和—with two-word phrases, one on each side of *and*.

The clumsiness is seen in *supervision maintenance*. Do we maintain supervision? Does supervision need to be maintained to begin with?

No. Absolutely not. But why *supervision maintenance* in the first place? It is all because of the attempt, consciously or unconsciously, to match the Chinese four-word pattern.

The above four-word structure has a fatal flaw in both meaning and structure. It is this flaw that causes the clumsiness in translation.

While 日常管理 (*routine management*) is structured as 日常 (*routine*) modifying 管理 (*management*), 监督维护 (*supervision maintenance*), because of its meaning, is not structured as such. 监督 (*supervision*) is not a modifier of 维护 (*maintenance*). Furthermore, 监督 and维护 are two verbs, each indicating a separate function. 监督 is not describing 维护.

With the two equally structured four-word phrases, the trap is set. What the linguist needs to avoid falling into it is to check the English version. If *supervision maintenance* doesn't sound right, then the linguist should break away from the pattern.

The correct rendition is, "Routine management, supervision, and maintenance of information flow."

Meaning overrules structure.

Summary Ending

According to Professor Bao, Middlebury Institute of International Studies at Monterey, "summary ending" includes words that simply rephrase what is already mentioned, as a summary.

Its linguistic function?

Well, it is a summary. No more or no less than rephrasing.

It is a unique Chinese sentence construction. There is no such thing in the English language. If translated, the "summary ending" words would be redundant, rendering a clumsy translation.

The linguist's job is to identify the summary ending, and skip it in translation.

Three telltale signs give away a summary ending:

First, the word preceding the summary ending is often a verb. The summary ending is trying to say, "All that is happening in the verb."

Second, when the word preceding the summary ending is not a verb, and it is translated, the English version reads redundantly.

Third, some words are the designated summary ending. They include 情况 (*situation*), 工作 (*work*), 关系 (*relationship*), and countless four-word phrases, with the last two words summarizing what the first two words already expressed.

- ✓ **Rule of Thumb No. 1:** If you can still get the exact message across without translating the summary ending, chances are you are dealing with one. Don't translate it.
- ✓ **Rule of Thumb No. 2:** The first line of defense is to check whether the translation makes sense. If not, something must be wrong. And that *something* is most likely the summary ending being translated.

Let's take a look at 情况:

➤ 请把你们的讨论情况跟我说说。
Redundancy: *Tell me about your discussion situation.*

The word 情况 is among the most frequently used summary endings. It doesn't mean situation (情况), nor does it serve any practical purpose. All it is saying is, "All that is going on in the discussion." So, "Tell me about your discussion" should work beautifully.

➤ 工程的进展情况如何?
Redundancy: *How is the progress situation of the project?*

Again, 进展 (progress) is itself a 情况 (situation). Progress situation sounds awkward. Proper translation should be, "How is the progress of the project?" Or "How is the project coming along?"

➤ 讲一讲新规则的执行情况
Redundancy: *Tell us about the implementation situation of the new regulations.*

In this case, *implementation* not only covers the part of how the new regulations were implemented, but 讲一讲 … 情况 can be taken care of by *tell us about* … So, the summary ending 情况 can be ignored.

Final translation: *Tell us about the implementation of the new regulations* (or *Tell us how the new regulations were implemented*).

Linguists are always fighting the guilt of missing words in translation, but translating the summary ending makes one just as guilty.

Use your best judgment. One effective way to decide whether you need to ignore the summary ending is to check the English version. If it sounds redundant or clumsy, chances are, you are seeing a summary ending.

Let's take a look at 工作 (*work*):

> 你们的准备工作怎么样了？
> Redundancy: *How is your preparation work coming along?*

Isn't *preparation* itself work? Put under the English-language-rule magnifier, *preparation work* is actually saying *preparation work work*. It doesn't flow.

Please note, 工作 in 政治工作 (political work), 日常工作 (routine work) is not a summary ending and should be translated. The telltale sign: the word preceding 工作 is not a verb. It is a modifier of 工作.

Well, sit tight. This is where 工作 gets interesting.

The linguist's judgment is being tested. In the case of 研究工作 (*research work*), 工作 can be both a summary ending (not to be translated) and *not* a summary ending (must be translated). It all depends on whether 研究 is a verb or a noun.

研究 as a verb: 工作 is a summary ending. Don't translate.

> 你们的研究工作进展如何？
> *How is your research going?*

Reason: 研究 (research) itself is work. Translating 工作 (*work*) would make it redundant.

研究 as a noun: 工作 is not a summary ending. Translate it.

> 你们为什么喜欢研究工作？
> *What attracts you to research work?*

Reason: 研究 (*research*) now functions as a modifier, much like "research paper," where *research* describes *paper*; or "research style," where *research* describe *style*; or "research institute," where *research* describes *institute*.

Now you get the idea.

Let's take a look at 关系:

> 良好的婚姻关系对一个家庭很重要
> Redundancy: *A good marriage relationship is important to a family.*

But isn't marriage a relationship already? People say "marriage" or "relationship" when they mean husband and wife but never the two together in one breath. They are the same thing.

The proper translation should be, "A good marriage is important to a family."

> 很多婚姻已不再是亲密关系，而是责任关系，义务关系，亲情关系。
> Redundancy: *Many marriages are no longer about intimacy relationship, but about responsibility relationship, obligation relationship, family relationship.*

The redundancy and clumsiness in the translation should raise a red flag. Take off the summary ending *relationship*, and the sentence flows smoothly, and the message is clear.

Translation: *Many marriages are no longer seeing intimacy; instead, they are about responsibility, obligation, and kinship.*

Not all 关系 are summary endings. The linguist needs to check whether the translation makes sense. While *marriage relationship* (婚姻关系) doesn't make sense, *buyer-seller relationship* (买卖关系) makes perfect sense, and so does *leader-subordinate relationship* (上下级关系).

Let's take a look at the summary ending in four-word phrases.

The most typical summary endings are found in many four-word phrases. When translated, the summary ending makes the translation awkward.

➤ 一个人的收入多少并不能决定他的幸福程度
Awkward translation: *One's high or low income cannot determine the degree of his happiness.*

Income has the idea of *high* or *low* built in it. Saying them again only messes up the message.

➤ 她很在意衣服的尺寸大小
Awkward translation: *She is very particular about the big or small size of her dress.*

Size itself, as a general idea, is about big or small. Unless one chooses to specify big size or small size, there is absolutely no need to spell out big or small for size.

➤ 如何判定车祸事故中的责任大小
Awkward translation: *How to determine big or small responsibilities for a car accident.*

Again, *responsibilities* include big ones and small ones. It is unnecessary to say them once more.

➤ 学生负担轻重与教学理念有关
Awkward translation: *Students' light or heavy burden has to do with the philosophy of teaching.*

The modifiers 轻重 (*light* or *heavy*) are part and parcel of 负担 (*burden*). Mention the word *burden*, and one can automatically think of *light* or *heavy*.

➤ 他在公司的待遇与他的职位高低无关
Awkward translation: *The treatment he receives in the company has nothing to do with high or low of his rank.*

Rank is used here in a general sense, not specifically high or low. So, *rank* alone is enough to indicate where he stands.

➤ 公司的待遇好坏很重要
Awkward translation: *A company's good or bad employee benefits are very important.*

Employee benefits is used here to refer to a condition. As such, it has all the elements in it: good, very good, not very good.

Now you get the picture.

A summary ending in four-word phrases can go on and on. It poses all kinds of challenges to linguists. Is it an idiom? Is it a summary-ending phrase? Do the last two words mean something?

Street Address

It is a delicate task. Chinese street address translation may be the few cases where English grammar doesn't matter much.

Look up Chinese and Western organizations in China on the Internet, and it's like opening a box of chocolates. "You never know what you're gonna get," to quote from the film *Forrest Gump*.

Some are completely in pinyin. Some go half pinyin and half English. Some go mostly pinyin with a word or two in English. If you are trying to find a standardized translation, good luck!

Even in pinyin, not all words are spelled correctly. Some leave a space between word groups. Some cramp them all together, with the first letter of the next word in upper case, assuming this would separate the words. And it does.

Now, it is your turn to translate a Chinese street address. Which approach do you take? Or better yet, which approach is correct?

- ✓ **Rule of Thumb No. 1:** Be consistent. If you translate one way with one address, do it with all other addresses.
- ✓ **Rule of Thumb No. 2:** Use the given address translation, no matter how strongly you don't like it. Chances are the local mail-delivery person matches what is on the envelope with what is on the door.
- ✓ **Rule of Thumb No. 3:** Minimize English translation. After all, your street address translation is meant for the local Chinese mail-delivery person to see. He or she reads pinyin far better than English.

Beyond the Rule of Thumb:

Translation is never a black-and-white, mathematically straightforward business. With all the rules available, one still finds it hard to negotiate the translation jungle.

When you are given different versions for the same address, use your best judgment.

The United States embassy in Beijing (北京市朝阳区安家楼55号) has one address, translated in two ways, with four different word choices:

➢ 55 Anjialou Rd, Chaoyang, Beijing China (US embassy website)
➢ No. 55 An Jia Lou Lu 100600 (US Department of State website)

The US embassy has *Rd* for 路, but the US Department of State has *Lu* for 路. The US embassy groups *Anjialou* (安家楼) together, but the US Department of State has *An Jia Lou*, all spaced out.

Conventions to Follow

Some street address translations are widely accepted. One can use them.

➢ 88 号(甲15号): No. 88 (Jia 15)
➢ 大道: Blvd (or Dadao)
➢ 大街: Street (or Dajie)
➢ 大厦: Building (or Dasha)
➢ 工业区: Industrial Zone
➢ 号: No. (as in No. 55)
➢ 胡同: Lane (or Hutong)
➢ 街: Street (or Jie)
➢ 经济开发区: Economic Development Zone

➢ 科技园: Tech Park
➢ 路: Road (or Lu)
➢ 区: District (as in Chaoyang District, Beijing)
➢ 三楼一门: Gate One, Building Three
➢ 省: Province
➢ 市: City
➢ 邮编: Postal Code

It is by no means an exhaustive list, but when in doubt, go pinyin.

Personal and Place Names

It is a relatively easy task. Here are the latest conventions to follow:

✓ **Rule of Thumb:** When in doubt, look it up on the Internet. If you find nothing, follow the three systems below.

Pinyin system:

Use pinyin for people with a mainland China background.
Format: Last name + First name, with no space between the two words, if it has two words.

Personal name:

邓小平 Deng Xiaoping
郭大年 Guo Danian
司马迁 Sima Qian
欧阳夏丹 Ouyang Xiadan
温洋 Wen Yang

Place name:

青岛 Qingdao
新疆 Xinjiang
西藏 Tibet
西安 Xi'an
陕西 Shaanxi

This pretty much covers all naming conventions.

There is no need to capitalize the last name (as in DENG Xiaoping) in an attempt to indicate it is a last name. The position says so. Nor is it necessary to hyphenate the first name (as in *Deng Xiao-ping*).

Wade-Jiles system:

Use the Wade-Jiles system to translate people's names outside mainland China.

If your reader is from place outside mainland China—say, Hong Kong, Taiwan, or Singapore, etc.—you need to use Wade-Jiles, but if your reader has a mainland China background, you need to use pinyin, as shown below:

Personal name:	*Place name:*
馬英九	台北
Wade-Jiles: Ma Ying-jeou	*Wade-Jiles:* Taipei
Pinyin: Ma Yingjiu	*Pinyin:* Taibei
蔡英文	台中
Wade-Jiles: Tsai Ing-wen	*Wade-Jiles:* Taichung
Pinyin: Cai Yingwen	*Pinyin:* Taizhong

Now you see. Not only is there a hyphen between the first name, but the spelling is somewhat different too. It is the Wade-Jiles system. Look it up on the Internet, and you will get the history.

De facto system:

There is no such system. I made it up.

The linguist needs to find the *de facto* translation first before translating a Chinese name. Any change to names would cause damage beyond the language realm.

马友友 has to be *Yo-yo Ma*, even if he is playing in China. The Chinese-English language media has to refer to him as such.

Imagine that *China Daily* writes his name as *Ma Youyou*. The rest of the world would be thrilled to notice that this *Ma* is playing as beautifully as that *Ma*.

Imaging again—*Tsingtao Beer* becomes *Qingdao Beer*. It would not be a change of just a few letters. The bottom line of the brewer might really drop to the bottom.

Use the commonly used version, and you will be safe.

"Honey, is there a split infinitive
in Chinese?"

Chapter 6

Where Translation May Go Funny--Informal Occasions

> Good translation should take into account the message, the intent of the author, the form of the message, and the need of the audience.
>
> -- Eugene Nida (American linguist, 1914–2011)

In This Chapter

✓ Greeting
✓ At the Dinner Table
✓ Seeing Friends Off
✓ Response to a Compliment

It is often easy to translate phrases that express formal, established ideas, like idioms, political jargon, economic terms, and even science words. There is a wealth of references. One can hardly go wrong.

But it is quite a different story, often a headache but always a challenge, when it comes to informal expressions. There are no established translations to use as a guide, but it helps to remember these rules of thumb.

- ✓ **Rule of Thumb No. 1:** Ask yourself, what would a native English speaker say in the same situation?
- ✓ **Rule of Thumb No. 2:** The translated version must see the same intended effect as the Chinese version does.

Informal expressions are particularly difficult to translate. They are figurative, humorous, and hard to find an exact match in the English language.

There are usually two scenarios in translation: One, there is an almost-the-same English expression, as in the case of

➤ 你今天脸色不错!
You look great today!

Two, the linguist translates the Chinese expression, only to have it come out funny—very funny—as in the case of

➤ 慢走! (as 1.4 billion Chinese would say when they see their guests off at the door)
Walk slowly!

Funny! Isn't it?

Why do people have to walk slowly? Did they drink too much? Or did they eat too much? Or is the road uneven?

Most likely, you would hear 慢走, even if you leave in a rush to catch the last bus. As many people have cars, the expression extends to 慢点开车! (*Drive slowly!*)

This is when the linguist has to think beyond the words.

Below are just a few scenarios where translation may go funny. To avoid this, the linguist must imagine what a native English speaker would say; otherwise, the translation would fail to have the same intended effect as the Chinese expression does.

Greeting

> 这一道够累的吧!
> Funny translation: *It must have been an exhausting trip!*

This is what Chinese people say first to the traveler after a long flight or drive, before the handshakes and hugs and patting on the backs.

I must add, this is a form of greeting, the Chinese way.

Imagine that a Chinese host greets his American guest at the airport with this affirmation: *You are tired!* This is not a greeting. This is telling me, *I had a lousy trip. I look tired.*

What does his American guest expect to hear as a greeting? What do Westerners say in the same situation? Definitely not "You must have had an exhausting trip!"

But 这一道够累的吧! is saying exactly that, or so you think.

What *is* the Chinese host really trying to say?

Well, the host is trying to greet you, for sure. But he greets in a Chinese way, showing that he cares about you. This is how 1.4 billion people greet each other at times like this. The greeting just doesn't come out the Western way—*So glad to see you!*

How do we translate 这一道够累的吧! in a way that gives the translated version the same intended effect as the Chinese version: a greeting? Or better yet, a greeting in disguise.

Translation: *I am so glad to see you! It must have been an exhausting trip!*

213

The greeting and care each get across beautifully. Beautifully, because the translation has the same intended effect to Western ears as it does to Chinese ears.

Did we add anything in translation? We did, with *I am so glad to see you!* Does that compromise the message? No. Not a bit. In fact, it saves the message: greeting.

A textbook case to support such an approach is the translation 不客气 in response to 谢谢. We translate 不客气 as "you are welcome" but not "don't be polite." Why? This is how English speakers respond to *thank you*.

Did we change a negative to a positive? We did, all for the purpose of getting the intended effect across. To do otherwise would fail the translation miserably.

Such is the principle of a good translation: *You are welcome* should have the same effect for English speakers as 不客气 would have for the Chinese.

At the Dinner Table

> 没什么好吃的, 凑合吃吧.
> Funny translation: *Nothing good to eat. Try to eat some.*

I guarantee you would hear it the moment you settle yourself into the chair at your host's dinner table, and the moment your host brings the last dish to the table, already loaded with piles of delicacies, and every moment in between.

How do you translate it? Exactly how it is said: *nothing good to eat?*

If so, every word is accounted for, but the intended message is lost by a big margin.

The intended message is actually, "I hope you like it!" But why the repeated "nothing good to eat"?

Well, it has to do with the Chinese culture of modesty. The Chinese guests have grown to understand the host's "nothing good to eat" as "I hope you like it."

So, logically, the translation should be, "I hope you like it."

Problem solved: both English speakers and the Chinese at the table will hear the same thing: *I hope you like it!*

Such is translation at its best.

Seeing Friends Off

> 慢走!
> Funny translation: *Walk slowly!*

As is mentioned briefly in the beginning, you would surely hear Chinese say *walk slowly* (or drive slowly 慢点开车) when they see friend off at the gate.

Why walk slowly? Again, one has to look beyond the words. Maybe in the old times, the road was uneven, and when it was dark, one indeed needed to walk slowly.

Fast forward to today. *Walk slowly* is still used, even though the road is even and streetlights light up every corner. When the Chinese say *walk slowly* now, they are actually saying good-bye (or *see you later* or *take care*).

So how do we translate the greeting 慢走?

Translation: "Bye-bye!" Or" See you!" Or "Bye! Take care!"—if you really want to translate 慢走.

215

Response to a Compliment

I guarantee that linguists, except those battle-tested ones, would hesitate a second or two when they hear Chinese respond to compliments and attempt to translate.

➢ To "I like your haircut," the Chinese would respond, 好什么呀，随便弄弄。
Nah. It's nothing. Just a simple cut.

➢ To "Your son is really smart," the Chinese would respond, 还聪明呀，就知道玩儿。
Nah. You should see him playing around all the time.

➢ To "Your voice is very good," the Chinese would respond, 咳，瞎唱。
Nah. Not really.

➢ To "You looked so great on stage," the Chinese would respond, 啊，还好看呀？
Are you kidding me?

The list can go on and on. Such responses are everywhere in all circumstances, but they all carry one common thread: deny your compliment—though pleasantly.

I must say, it is the culture of modesty at its best. These "nahs" are not heard as a denial to Chinese ears. They are, in fact, the Chinese way of saying, "Thank you. I hear you. I am glad you noticed!"

Translation is a cross-culture business. If Chinese ears hear "Thank you. I am glad you noticed," the translation should make it sound the same to Western ears, shouldn't it?

In order for the Chinese responses to do the same trick for Westerners, the linguist needs to twist them a bit. It's simple. All the linguist needs to do is add "thank you" and then move on to translate those pleasantly toned denials, just to make sure the modesty part is not lost.

We have the two cultures covered nicely.

"Do we read from left to right, top down
or from right to left?"

Chapter 7

Say It Properly

> In translation, messages get lost not because the linguist fails to follow the rules, but because there are always exceptions. Solution? Use logic and common sense.
>
> --温 洋 Wen Yang (US historian and linguist, 1956 -)

In This Chapter:

- ✓ **Present Tense or Past Tense**
- ✓ **Plural or Singular**
- ✓ **Correct Use of *The***
- ✓ **Culturally Loaded Expressions**
- ✓ **Conditioned by the Chinese Wording**

Years ago, I was showing James, my linguist colleague at SAIC, an English translation I did for a Chinese expression. "I know what you are trying to say," he said, after going over my translation a couple of times, "but we don't say it this way."

The *way*, I believe, is the proper use of the English words.

Translating Chinese into English is, in a sense, rewriting the expressions in English. So what comes out should make James say, "That's how we say it."

Easily said. A linguist faces countless choices before he/she lands that *that's-how-we-say-it* translation. And it is particularly difficult for non-native English-speaking linguists.

It is difficult because the linguist is fighting a battle on two fronts: keeping eyes wide open for proper English usage and resisting the temptation to mimic improper usage by native English speakers, blinded by the assumption that if it is from a native speaker, it must be correct and proper.

No. Not always. Haven't we all heard native English speakers say, "reverse back"; "repeat again"; "there's ten of us"; "it ain't nothing"; "I left it outside of the building"; and the like.

In translation, words should be used properly.

Below are a few examples, among millions, to show how, by a slip of the pen, a translation can go wrong.

Present Tense or Past Tense

Case No. 1: Did you know?

Tenses are the first thing we learn in grammar classes. It doesn't seem to be a problem, until it comes to translating 你知道 … 吗?

Is it *Do you know …?* Or *Did you know …?*

It is all in the tense. One day, on our routine ice cream trip to CVS, my good friend and colleague Caleb explained the difference, after running it through various contexts.

✓ When you ask "Do you know …?" you actually don't know the answer. You want to know.

220

✓ When you ask "Did you know …?" you already know the answer. You just want to tell the other person by posing a question.

Translating 你知道 … 吗? in present tense or past tense gets a different message across. Let me put 你知道 … 吗? in perspective.

➤ 你知道她明天要走吗?

Do you know if she is leaving tomorrow? (You don't know it. You want the other person to give you some information.)

Or

Did you know she is leaving tomorrow? (You know she is leaving. You want to tell the other person about her leaving.)

Chinese language has a clever way of distinguishing the two, not by tense but by structure: 你知道吗? 她明天要走了. This is clearly, "I know. You don't know. Let me tell you."

If 你知道吗? 她明天要走了 is translated in present tense, the intended *I-already-knew* message will be lost. If it is an everyday conversation, nothing significant is lost. People may quickly know who already knew what in subsequent conversations.

What if you are in an FBI field office, translating a taped conversation involving a crime? The FBI wants to know whether Suspect Wang already knew who killed Mrs. Zhang.

In the tape, Suspect Wang is heard asking someone: "你知道是谁杀的张太太吗?"

What tense do you use? "Do you know…?" or "Did you know…?" The difference in tense may translate life or death.

Case No. 2: Historical Present Tense

Not all past events must be recounted in the past tense.

There is what English grammar calls "historical present tense." You are recounting a past event, but you are doing it in the present tense.

One can often hear on the radio recounts of past events, all done in the present tense. Next time a story comes on the radio, try to hear the tense.

A good example is Jan Wong's *Beijing Confidential*. The book is about her trip to Beijing to find her long-lost friends. It all happened years ago, but it is told in present tense.

The beauty of this present tense usage is that you make everything sound as though it's happening right now, right in front of you. Armed with this understanding, the linguist can make an educated choice to use the present tense when translating a story from the past, in spite of the Chinese past tense marker 了.

Plural or Singular

Chinese nouns don't carry a distinct plural or singular form. They all look singular. It is up to the linguist to decide which form to use.

This section is not about changing child to children, fish to fishes, money to moneys, sky to skies, or rain to rains when it comes to 孩子, 鱼, 钱, 天, 雨. There are already tons of grammar books on this subject.

In these cases, both singular and plural forms mean basically the same thing. The linguist won't have a headache in translating them.

Rather, this section is about three other issues:

1. The meaning changes completely if the linguist translates a noun to a plural form.

2. A singular noun refers to a category, while a plural indicates general reference. The linguist must make a choice.

3. Improper English.

Issue No.1: The meaning is changed.

It's never the case in Chinese. How can a word change its meaning if you make it a plural? 一次讨论 and 十次讨论 are both "discussion." So is one machine and a hundred machines. But translation involves a different language. The linguist seriously must take into account what happens in that language.

Let's take a look at these translations.

➢ 通讯设备: Is it *communication equipment* or *communications equipment?*

Simply put, *communication* (singular) is about interaction between people; namely, talking, chatting, gossiping, exchanging ideas. *Communications* (plural) is about technology, devices, and equipment that transmits news and ideas, like TV, radio, wires, cables, sound systems, and satellites.

Luckily, in Chinese, 通讯 is not used for talking, gossiping, and chatting. It is exclusively reserved for technology. Even so, the linguist is still not free from mistranslating 通讯.

➢ 张先生是通讯专家, 有问题就找他.
Mr. Zhang is a communication expert. He is our go-to guy for any issues.

Or

Mr. Zhang is a communications expert. He is our go-to guy for any issues.

The first translation, with *communication expert,* is saying that Mr. Zhang knows how to communicate with people. If you don't know how to talk to people, ask him for advice.

The second translation, with *communications expert,* is saying that Mr. Zhang is a technician. If you have any technical issues, ask him for help.

See the difference an *s* makes?

Similarly, 通讯设备, 通讯系统, 通讯物资, 雷达通讯系统 and so forth should all carry a plural *communications.*

It may be particularly challenging for linguists whose mother tongue is Chinese. They have to make an extra effort to use plural forms where necessary, much like they must remember to specify *he* or *she* when speaking English.

The reason is simple. There is only *Ta* in spoken (not in written) Chinese to cover both sexes. It is not in their linguistic DNA to say *he* or *she.*

➢ 经验: Is it *experience* or *experiences?*

Does a plural *experiences* mean more 经验? Unfortunately, no. 经验 is experience (singular), whereas 经历 is *experiences* (plural).

In other words, *experience* (singular) is about skill, expertise, and knowledge. *Experiences* (plural) means things that have happened to you in the past.

Adding an *s* to *experience* doesn't make it more 经验. Translation for 在这方面, 我有更多的经验 should be "I have more experience dealing with it."

These are only two of many such cases. But the principle remains the same. Always ask yourself, should this be singular or plural? Chances are you may embarrass yourself if you use the wrong form.

Issue No.2: Is it a category (singular) or general reference (plural)?

Again, all Chinese words stand singular, until you add a plural modifier in front of the word, such as 很多, 几个, and so forth. The sense of category or general reference is all implied in the context. Such is not the case in English. The linguist needs to know, from the context, which form to use.

Let's take a look.

> 有问题吗?
>
> Do you have any questions?

Or

> Is there any question?

The first translation, with *questions*, suggests that the person asking the question assumes there are many questions—questions in general.

The second translation, with *question*, is trying to say, "Is there any doubt?" or "Do you question it?"

But how do Chinese express the category 问题, since both category and general reference all take a singular form 问题? Most likely, the speaker would put a stress on 问题.

> 我弹钢琴
>
> I play piano.

Piano (singular) is treated as a category of musical instrument, as opposed to guitar, violin, flute, and so forth

> 我们商店卖钢琴
>
> We sell pianos.

Pianos (plural) is treated as various models—upright, grand, keyboards. Pianos in general.

By the same logic, 你喜欢椅子还是沙发? is apparently about category. Both 椅子 and 沙发 should be rendered in singular form: *chair* and *sofa*.

A good example of such distinctions is found in military actions. In combat operations, people must distinguish *friend or foe* (分清敌我). It is never *friends or foes*, because we are talking about category (singular), not about how many (plural).

Again, we say *tank* unit, never *tanks* unit; *bread* basket, never *breads* basket; *cup* holder, never *cups* holder. They are all about category.

Of course, conventional grammar also holds that when a noun modifies another noun, the modifier takes a singular form.

On an airplane, we often hear flight attendants politely ask passengers, "Tea or coffee?" But never "Teas or coffees?" It is a choice of a category, not choices of each.

Maybe, in the not-so-distant future, when the flight attendant comes up to you with a tray of teas of all flavors and coffees from all over the world, you would hear, 茶还是咖啡? And you would translate as, "Teas or coffees?", suggesting not only category but also choices within each category.

Issue No. 3: Improper usage

- ✓ *in detail* (correct)
- ✓ *in details* (wrong)
- ✓ *in depth* (correct)
- ✓ *in depths* (wrong)

What is the translation for 她作了详细的解释?

✓ She explained *the details, or*
✓ She explained *in detail*

First of all, *in details* is incorrect. It is not an adverb. Second, it doesn't mean more details.

In fact, the phrase *in detail* functions as an adverb, like *in silence, in depth, in the world, in anger.* It is an adverb phrase.

To suggest more details, you can say, *in great detail* (singular). Again, not *in great details* (plural). *In details* doesn't mean more details.

Similarly, *in depth* serves as an adverb, as in, *He talked about the subject in depth.*

Making it *in depths* (plural) doesn't make it deeper. It makes you look funny.

To suggest more details, you can say, "Tell me the details," or "She explains the details."

To suggest something deeper, you can say, "I want to thank you from the depths of my heart."

Correct Use of *The*

Overuse of *the* is common among linguists whose first language is Chinese.

I am not trying to address the use of *the* in a general sense. Look it up on the Internet (or in a library), and you will find tons of helpful information on how to use *the* correctly.

Since the first day in grammar school, we have been told and reminded, time and again, that *the* is for specific reference.

But it remains a beautiful theory until one comes into contact with a specific translation.

Take a look at the following conversation:

Q: 你打篮球吗?
Do you play basketball? (**general reference**)

A: 打.
Yes.

Q: 你打什么位置?
What position do you play?

A: 中锋
The center. (**specific reference**)

There is no hint whatsoever of *the* in Chinese. But in translation, one has to make a choice.

Without *the*, basketball is referred to as a general category of sports.

With *the*, 中锋 is treated as a specific position, as opposed to the point guard, the shooting guard, and the two forwards.

When we read, 篮球首次被介绍到中国是1896 年 (*The game of basketball was first introduced to China in 1896.*)

This time, 篮球 takes *the*, because the game is treated as a specific sport, as opposed to baseball, tennis, and other sports.

Such is the use of *the* in a nutshell.

Let's take a look at the second case of overuse of *the*.

In an introduction or abstract of an article, the subject being introduced often appears in the beginning of the first words, such as

✓ 手机是二十世纪的一大发明
✓ 电脑改变了人的生活

✓ 宠物狗是都市的一个新现象
✓ 光纤通讯技术不同于传统通讯技术

But often, the translation would read

✓ The cell phone …
✓ The computer …
✓ The pet dog …
✓ The fiber-optic communications …

Why all the uses of *the*? All of those four subjects are general reference.

Sometimes, the distinction is not so black-and-white. The linguist still needs to read into the context to determine a specific reference from a general one.

And that is why proper use of *the* is still—and always will be—a challenge to many linguists, especially those non-native English speakers.

Culturally Loaded Expressions

Again, I am not talking about idioms, slang, popular sayings, and the like. There is already a wealth of literature on these subjects.

I am after those words that are explained one way in dictionaries but mean something else in real life. The translation will definitely fail if the linguist follows the dictionaries.

These words are often culturally conditioned. They mean one thing in one culture but something else in another. In this case, the linguist must think beyond dictionaries and across culture lines to find that perfect translation.

Below are two typical examples to illustrate the point.

Example No. 1: 龙 (*Dragon*)

A good example is the translation of 龙. Dragon. Right? Yes and no.

As an animal, fictional or real, 龙 is indeed *dragon*. But as a cultural symbol, where it is revered, dragon lives beyond the animal kingdom. Elsewhere, its symbolism is lost.

When Taiwan, Hong Kong, Singapore, and South Korea were hailed as 亚洲四小龙, the translation is *Four Tigers*, not *Four Dragons*.

The reason is cultural. *Dragon*, in the West, is seen as a monster. Not a positive image. Saying that the four economic powerhouses are dragons is like saying they are bad, even with their economic successes. Not only is it a bad translation, but it is also irresponsible.

Example No. 2: coward (懦弱者, 胆小鬼)

Let's do a reverse translation to drive the message home.

On March 6, 2008, a US Armed Forces recruiting station in Times Square, New York City, was bombed. Mayor Bloomberg had the following to say: "Whoever the coward is, we will find him."

Coward is explained as 懦弱者, 胆小鬼 in 韦氏高阶美语–英汉双解词典 (*Random House Webster's Dictionary of American English*). And by extension, 现代汉语词典 (*Modern Chinese Language Dictionary*) runs two definitions under 懦弱: 软弱胆小的人; 软弱, 不坚强, all meaning *weak, lack of bravery, not strong*.

Should the linguist translate *coward* to 懦弱, 软弱胆小的人, according to dictionary definitions?

Is the bomber a 软弱胆小的人 (*weak, lacking bravery*)? In fact, in many such attacks, including the 9/11 attacks in 2001, the London bombings on July 7, 2005, and the Paris attacks in November 2015, the terrorists all were called *cowards* and their attacks *cowardly*.

The Chinese language logic would argue that the terrorists actually were brave, weren't they? They dared to risk their lives. They were not 软弱胆小的人 by any definition, the Chinese way.

Something is missing in the translation. And that *something* is the cultural interpretation of *coward* in English and its translation 软弱胆小 (*weak, lacking bravery*) in Chinese.

Westerners and Chinese interpret *coward* (or *cowardly*) and 懦弱, 胆小 differently. In the case of terrorist attacks, the West sees the *coward* in the terrorists' fear of fighting people of equal or stronger power, such as police and soldiers. Therefore, they are *cowards*.

The Chinese see fear-no-death acts in the terrorists' bombings. Therefore, they are not 懦弱, 胆小, as the dictionary has it.

Thus, the translation fails.

For the West's idea of *coward*, the Chinese language has another term: 卑鄙 (*mean, shameless, spineless*). To get the correct message across to Chinese ears, *coward* (or *cowardly*) should be translated as such. This way, both *coward* and 卑鄙 are saying the same thing, with the same denunciating power.

Conditioned by the Chinese Wording Logic

How a linguist chooses English words depends a lot on the Chinese words he/she sees. This, in turn, determines whether the linguist says it the English way. It affects his/her word choices too.

This is often the case where linguists are conditioned by the Chinese wording, like it or not. Don't we all have the same experiences at some point in translation? When we see 用, we immediately choose *use* from our mental database.

When we see 我不能用鼻子喘气, the translation is automatically, "I can't use my nose to breathe." We have a perfect match, verb for verb, noun for noun, and even the word order.

Nothing wrong with that.

This conditioning, however, often stops the linguist from finding other ways to say the same thing, ways that may give the linguist more choices and make the translation colloquial.

How about "I can't breathe through my nose"? Apparently, that's a more colloquial version, but it doesn't come to mind quickly. Why? The linguist can't find *through* in the Chinese sentence. The word-matching mode doesn't lead to the word *through*.

I can be absolutely sure, if the Chinese wording changes to 通过 鼻子喘气, that the translation would be "breathe through my nose." But it is not colloquial Chinese. Hardly anyone says it this way.

Let's take a look at another case.

When we see 因为, we immediately think of *because*. How about the following 因为?

"Instead, largely thanks to the Iraq War, Rumsfeld will go down history as an arrogant manager who ruined American reputation by allowing abuses at Abu Ghraib prison"(*Newsweek,* 11/19/2006).

Had this been a Chinese article, would the linguist translate 因为 to "thanks to"? I doubt it. The linguist may be conditioned to link 因为 with *because*, and *thanks* with 谢谢, without much thought to the *to* that follows.

It may be a matter of personal style, but wouldn't it be better to have more choices? What stands in the way is the conditioning mechanism that prevents the linguist from thinking beyond the word he/she sees.

The following wording is particularly challenging, almost impossible, for Chinese linguists to come up with.

✓ *Tom is a hard person to reach.* (Tom 很难找到)
✓ *Love is a terrible thing to take lightly.* (不能把爱情当儿戏)
✓ *Time is a terrible thing to waste.* (时间浪费不得)

For a native Chinese linguist, it is inconceivable to express the above ideas beginning with "Tom is a hard ..."; "Love is terrible ..."; "Time is terrible ..." The Chinese wording logic would not allow one to think of it this way. How can love be terrible? Treating it lightly is terrible.

There is nothing wrong in saying, "It is a terrible thing to take love lightly." But don't colloquial expressions add to the variety and flavor of the translation?

Next time, before doing a quick word association (*use* for 用, for example), ask yourself, *Are there better ways?*

Chances are, there are.

Good luck!

Index

Made in the USA
Middletown, DE
14 March 2018